BEN MUSGRAVE

Ben Musgrave grew up in the UK, Bangladesh and India. *Pretend You Have Big Buildings* is his professional debut. He is currently under commission to the National Theatre Studio.

Ben Musgrave

PRETEND YOU HAVE
BIG BUILDINGS

NICK HERN BOOKS

London

www.nickhernbooks.co.uk

A Nick Hern Book

Pretend You Have Big Buildings first published in Great Britain
as a paperback original in 2007 by Nick Hern Books Limited,
14 Larden Road, London W3 7ST

Pretend You Have Big Buildings copyright © 2007 Ben Musgrave

Ben Musgrave has asserted his right to be identified as the author
of this work

Cover image: photography by Jonathan Oakes, design by
Reform Creative

Cover design: Ned Hoste, 2H

Typeset by Country Setting, Kingsdown, Kent CT14 8ES
Printed and bound in Great Britain by Biddles, King's Lynn, Norfolk

A CIP catalogue record for this book is available from
the British Library

ISBN   978 1 85459 992 6

Pretend You Have Big Buildings was first performed at the Royal Exchange Theatre, Manchester, on 11 July 2007, with the following cast:

DANNY	Sacha Dhawan
LEON	Jonathan Bailey
RUKHSANA	Shobna Gulati
ROB	Steve North
KAREN	Tanya Franks
STEVEN	Billy Seymour
ANNIE	Susan Twist

Directors   Sarah Frankcom and Jo Combes
Designer   Jaimie Todd
Lighting Designer   David Holmes
Sound Designer   Ian Dickinson

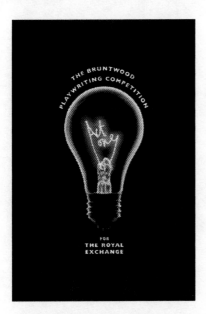

Bruntwood
Playwriting Competition

North West Property Company, Bruntwood, launched the Bruntwood Playwriting Competition for the Royal Exchange in 2005 with the aim of discovering and celebrating the UK's writing talent of the future. With a prize fund of £45,000, the competition has established itself as the only national playwriting competition in the UK and the largest of its kind in British theatre.

The prestigious judging panel was chaired by former Secretary of State for Culture, Media and Sport, the Rt Hon Lord Smith of Finsbury, and included actress Brenda Blethyn OBE, actor and playwright Kwame Kwei-Armah, National Theatre Artistic Director Nicholas Hytner, Royal Exchange Artistic Director Braham Murray and Chairman of Bruntwood and High Sheriff of Greater Manchester Michael Oglesby DL.

Ben Musgrave's winning script was chosen from nearly 2,000 entries, and his play premiered at the Royal Exchange Theatre, in the main space, as part of the inaugural Manchester International Festival, of which Bruntwood were sponsors.

www.bruntwood.co.uk

www.royalexchange.co.uk

PRETEND YOU HAVE BIG BUILDINGS

Ben Musgrave

Acknowledgments

Pretend You Have Big Buildings began life during my MA in Writing for Performance at Goldsmiths College in 2005, and I am indebted to the MA group: Eric Bland, Duncan Chalmers, Jodi Gray, Kenny Emson and Pip Mayo; to Deborah Paige, who conducted a fruitful initial workshop; and especially to John Ginman, whose expert dramaturgy guided the play to its first incarnation at BAC in July 2005. Later, Act One was staged by acting students from E15 at the Actors Centre in 2006, and I am very grateful to them (and to Caroline Eves and Abigail Gonda for the opportunity), but especially to Meriel Baistow-Clare, who directed the play, and whose work on the script set the scene for the next phase of development. I would like to thank the Dog House Group for their support, rigour and friendship: Robin Booth, Lucy Caldwell, Nick Harrop, Matt Morrison, Jennifer Tuckett, Paul Amman Brar. And many thanks also to those who have read and discussed the script with me: Steve King, Lucy Morrison, Ben Jancovich, Chris Hannan, Nicholas Hytner, Jenny Marshall, Billy Dosanjh.

Thanks to Alex Marshall and Mark Willingham for development of the Essexman routines. To Ioannis Iordanidis, Amanda Washbrook, and Alex Haughey for advice on motorbikes. To the late Jim Reed for technical support. To all at Havering Libraries, especially Simon Donaghue for introducing me to local history. To Skye Wheeler. To Nick Hern and all at Nick Hern Books. To Mel Kenyon. To my parents.

And of course to Bruntwood and the Royal Exchange, without whom none of this extraordinary business would have come about. Finally, and especially, to Jo Combes and Sarah Frankcom, whose exemplary stewardship of the play's development has brought the script on no end.

Historical Note

Havering Council built the Dolphin, the swimming pool referred to by the characters, in the eighties. Its distinctive pyramidal roof – which looked a little like the top of Canary Wharf – was the most remarkable architectural feature of Romford town centre. When pieces of roof panelling began to fall off, the pool was closed down, and remained derelict for ten years. In 2003, the Dolphin was finally razed to the ground, and an enormous ASDA began to take shape.

Notes on the Text

A new line indicates a new impulse of thought or speech, and may replace a comma.

A blank line within speech generally replaces a beat.

A forward slash [/] indicates the point at which the next designated speech begins.

Italics within speech indicate added emphasis, (*except when in parentheses*, which indicate a stage direction).

However, speech within parentheses is generally to be regarded as internal – or at any rate exclusive of other characters in the scene.

Characters

DANNY, *fifteen, mixed heritage*

LEON, *fifteen, white, Essex*

RUKHSANA, *thirty-seven, Indian*

ROB, *forty, white, Essex*

KAREN, *forty, white, Essex*

STEVEN, *fifteen, white, Essex*

ANNIE, *forty-two, white, Essex*

Various recorded voices

Act One *takes place in November to mid-December 1995.*

Act Two *takes place in the hours after Act One.*

This text went to press before the end of rehearsals and may differ slightly from the play as performed.

ACT ONE: Canary Wharf

Scene One

Pretend You Have Big Buildings

An aeroplane.

RUKHSANA *and* DANNY, *side by side.*

DANNY *looks out of the window. He generally addresses the landscape.*

DANNY   Hey, London

               RUKHSANA *holds a claret UK passport. She generally addresses the audience.*

RUKHSANA   Look of this, this

DANNY   (*To the landscape.*) Look at you
               The light on the loop of the river

RUKHSANA   And the embassy took his.
               Yours. Yours.
               They took it away
               I remember the picture but it's
               Fading it's all dammed up in my head

DANNY   The Thames

               The PILOT *makes an announcement.*

PILOT'S VOICE
               It's a bit chilly down on the ground, ladies and
                  gents, about three degrees Celsius

RUKHSANA   Oh my God

PILOT'S VOICE
               And quite a strong north wind so / do

DANNY   (*Imitating the* PILOT.)
               'Do wrap up warm, ladies and gents.'
               Do wrap up warm.
               Or you won't know what's hit you.

               DANNY *looks out of the window.*

RUKHSANA   And there's a list of things I have to remember.
            Just to get us from the airport.
            Things about staying calm and being strong and
                not being offended by coldness

DANNY   And England.
            From the way you're looking
            From the sky over the coast so green . . . !
            I think you're going to be just right.

            A judder of violent turbulence. RUKHSANA
            reacts badly.

            Mum
            It's normal

RUKHSANA   We're falling?

DANNY   It's perfectly normal.
            He'll announce it. Like this:
            'Just a spot of turbulence, ladies and gentlemen'
            With his English voice.
            Look at you.
            Like you've never been on a plane before.
            Sweating.

PILOT'S VOICE
            Just entering a patch of turbulence there, ladies
                and gents, we should be clear shortly.

RUKHSANA   (*To the audience.*)
            I know where I'm going no more
            Than the poor bastards to my right.
            The wide-eyed family in their best clothes
            Who packed their lunch in Bombay
            And eat it with their hands.

            The lights flicker out. The plane is landing.

DANNY   Hold my hand

RUKHSANA   Are we landing?

DANNY   Yes. We're landing.

            She holds his hand. The plane touches down.

RUKHSANA   And this family
            They will have relations waiting
            Seven little cousins
            Waving
            Miraculous placards
            And I have no placard.

6

Only this strange son
Who's dreamed of this day for fifteen years.
Who thinks he knows
How to hail a taxi.

ROB *stands by the Canary Wharf Tower. By his
car. A smart suit. He speaks as if to a companion.*

ROB   I tell you
I can't take my eyes off that!
And by Christmas they reckon all the office space
    will be taken
And all the lights turned on again.
The company's just moved the HQ right up there.
And they got all of us supervisors, the white-
    collars and that, they brought us all in to talk
    about the future.
They ask me what I think of the new locale.
I say, (*A joke.*) 'Well it's not small'
They laugh
(*A cheeky smile.*) 'It's not small'
This bloke says: 'D'you know how big it is?'
'No.'
'It's taller than the Telecom Tower.
It's taller than the *Natwest* Tower.'
(*A cheeky nonchalance.*) 'Oh yeah?'
'It's the *tallest* structure in the *country*.'
(*Coolly.*) 'Oh yeah?'
Nice and cool. Don't give it away. Don't give
    nothing away.
'Fucking stupid name for a tower,' I proceed,
    'Canary Wharf'.

RUKHSANA *and* DANNY *are now in a taxi
zooming east. They gaze out of the window.*

DANNY   Look at it.

RUKHSANA   And the roads are smooth here, Danny, you'll
    notice that and nobody uses their horn so the
    roads are quiet and

DANNY   It's

RUKHSANA   And at this stage of a city it always looks like this

DANNY   Concrete and pebbledash

RUKHSANA   (*To the audience.*) And now I remember it.
On the fringes it's
Mock Tudor and red-brick

7

	Business parks and tunnels. But soon we hit the heart. The centre.
ROB	Course I was burning ta say 'I was born two minutes walk away from here.' I was actually born *two minutes* away from the *tallest* structure in the *country*.
RUKHSANA	Look at that!
	It is Canary Wharf. DANNY is impressed.
DANNY	Is it near here?
RUKHSANA	Maybe.
DANNY	I hope it's near here.
	ROB is still at Canary Wharf.
ROB	And our house. All gone. Wiped away. Pwwwhhht. And up comes this fackin (*Tower.*) This I mean I'm not a socialist I'm not sayin I mean it sure as fuck's an improvement but what I wanna know is Who's been made the mug in all this?
	Relax. He gets his keys out and zaps the remote locking system. The car makes its unlocking sound and light. He gets in.
	Remote Central-locking.
	He puts on a pair of chamois gloves, and some driving glasses.
	He shuts the door.
	Electric Windows.
	He puts on some music, which continues to the end of the scene.
	CD Player, *as standard*.
	On the passenger seat is a bag from an expensive shopping boutique.
	And something for the lady.
	Ignition. His car growls into life. He zooms off.
DANNY	Is this right?

RUKHSANA   What?

DANNY   (*To the taxi driver.*) Excuse me

RUKHSANA   Relax.

DANNY   Excuse me, we've moved past the centre.

           That sign that green sign
           It says we're headed east.
           Excuse me.

TAXI DRIVER'S VOICE
           It's Romford you're going?

RUKHSANA   Yes.

TAXI DRIVER'S VOICE
           Well, that's about as far east as you can get, mate.

           ROB is driving east. He loosens his tie.

ROB   Royal Hospital on the right. St Clem's. Where
               Leon was born.
           Which was just before
           (*A complicated manoeuvre.*)
           Excuse me
           It's a 'mare this.
           Just before we moved out to Romford.
           Nah, it weren't too bad growing up in the East
               End. It was a good community spirit.
           But, er
           Well things change, don't they?
           The people change.

           Something up on the road.

           Here we go . . .
           (*To an errant motorist.*)
           Come on, mate.
           Are you going?
           YOU GONNA BE A PRAT ALL YER LIFE?
           Well GO then!
           Dickhead fucking dickhead.

           ROB beeps his horn. He can't take it any more.

           This isn't the fucking day for this.

DANNY   I don't believe it. Did you know?

RUKHSANA   No.

DANNY   He said

RUKHSANA   He never showed me!

DANNY   He said it is always warmer, it is always warmer
            in the centre of the city.

            ROB *is now at Forest Gate.*

ROB   West Ham down there.
            Funnily enough. Funnily enough
            You do not see a white face round there except
            on a match day.

RUKHSANA   Never showed me any of this.

ROB   I don't have a problem. That was how I was raised.
            Now one of the guys who spoke to us today. One
            of the big boys
            He was an Asian fella as it goes
            But he had *Really*
            Really Good English.
            Not like some of the coloured boys on the floor.
            Oh no.
            He was marbles-in-his-mouth, you know?
            Well dressed:
            (*He taps his breast pocket.*) Ralph Lauren.
            Pockmarked face like some of them have
            But Really Good English.
            (*A cheeky smile.*) And he's called Nathaniel,
            right . . . *Nathaniel.*

            The taxi screeches to a halt at the lights.

DANNY   And after all he said

ROB   And there is a moment.

DANNY   After all those stories

ROB   And we're coming up to it. Just past the tollgate.
            Just after the point where the London Road meets
            Whalebone Lane:
            A farm.
            A strip of countryside that stretches north to south.
            It's the end of London. And this is Romford.

RUKHSANA   This is what you are.

ROB   It don't last long

            LEON *enters. The Dolphin appears, a pyramidal
            structure housing a broken-down swimming pool.
            He speaks directly to the audience.*

LEON   But just pretend

ROB	The roundabouts, the ring road, the swimming pool they built and closed down
LEON	Just pretend you havvem
ROB	This is it.
LEON	That you got the big buildings that make you proud
ROB	This is where we moved. This is where we can breathe. Raise a family.

ROB *stops his car, and gets out.*

LEON	Just lie.
	Just dream. It don't matter.

Fuckin pretend it
One day, in nineteen ninety-five, it came out that shithole swimming pool
That broken down swimming pool they called the Dolphin
That pyramid they built and closed down
It burst outta there.
Like you know one of those fairy-tale oak trees:
Romford Castle
Like someone had wished it, you know?

Pretend
Just pretend. There's no harm I swear
That it cracked through dirty glass, asbestos, corrugated steel.
Romford Castle
Cutting off the ring road.
This massive tower and a moat that joined the river
Lovely.
Our own
Proper
Fuck-off
Castle.

Scene Two

Man and Boy

LEON *and* ROB. *The living room of* ROB*'s house. They are both nervous.*

LEON	How'd it go?
	Did you give em what for?
	Did you fuck em over?

ROB	One minute.
LEON	Did you come out laughin?
ROB	Leon. Uno minuto. Where's your mother?
LEON	She's out.
	With friends, she said.
	She won't be long.
ROB	She alright today, is she?
LEON	Yeah.
ROB	She OK?
LEON	Oh yeah, she was chattin away. No problem.
ROB	She had her tea?
LEON	Sort of.
ROB	Here we go.
LEON	Nah – I put cheese 'n' ham toast on, right?
ROB	Oh no.
LEON	For her birthday!
ROB	I thought I could smell something burnin.
LEON	Dint burn too bad.
ROB	What are you two like?
LEON	(*Over-defensive.*) What have I done?
ROB	Nothing.
	Beat.
LEON	What's that, then? (*In the bag.*)
ROB	For her birthday.
	He pulls an expensive dress from the bag.
	It's what she wanted.
LEON	Let's have a look then?
	LEON *examines it.*
	No, it's nice. It's nice.
ROB	So you gonna behave yerself tonight?
LEON	Course I am.

ROB	Pictures with Steven?
LEON	Yeah.
ROB	Because your mum and me, we're going out tonight.
LEON	I know.
ROB	I don't want a repeat of last time.
LEON	Shut up, man
ROB	*Don't* / you
LEON	Just / leave it
ROB	Tell me / what to say
LEON	So are they gonna sack you all then?
ROB	Oh fuckssake, Leon Don't ask me Don't ask me.
LEON	What did you tell them?
ROB	Ar
LEON	Well?
ROB	(*Explodes*.) I told those wankers Head-office papershufflers I said 'We shouldn't even be discussing this. It's ridiculous we're even discussing this.'
LEON	That's right!
ROB	'And it's not just us who gets fucked if we take the package. There's hundreds who'll lose their jobs if we give way. You know – black *and* white. And not just the boys on the floor. The whole supply chain.'
LEON	That's right.
ROB	It's all joined up. This bloke Nathaniel come in. Brown-skinned, but you can tell he's money. 'You take redundancy now, it'll be easier in the long term. We could lay before you some very interesting offers.'

I say, 'How long have you been in this country,
　　　Nathaniel?'
Coz I
I gave this *company* twenty years of my life.'
He turns to me. Looks me right in the eyes. Smiles.
'We've already structured very attractive terms
For those in long service
Who voluntarily accept the redundancy package.'

But then the union guys take over and we just
　　　have to sit there.

And Nathaniel comes back.
'Gents . . . do you want the good news or the bad
　　　news?'

Pause. OK.

'We're not going to make anyone redundant, for
　　　the moment.'

LEON　　　　　Fuckin A!

ROB　　　　　And we're nearly jumpin up an down, Lee, we
　　　　　　　　think we're laughin then he goes
　　　　　　　'Here's the bad news.'

Four-day week. Even supervisors.

No more overtime.

We're taking a pay cut.
We had to sign it.

I ain't gonna let it go, Lee!
This is your job in three, four years' time.
If we can just hang on, fings'll perk up.
This is your future. I want you
To have a future.

They don't hug.

Scene Three

Hot Water

*That evening. A lounge/kitchen, Romford, in darkness. ANNIE,
DANNY's aunt, is showing RUKHSANA and DANNY the house.
ANNIE wears motorbike leathers, and has placed her helmet
close by her. There is a basin in the room, a trunk and a few other
packing boxes lying around.*

ANNIE slowly increases the intensity of the light.

ANNIE	That's the dimmer switch there.
	That lets you change the brightness.
	He was good with wires that much I'll say for him.
	He did it all when he was seventeen. Rigged it all up.
	Saved her a fortune.
	Well, don't just stand there, come in.
	But mind out for the boxes.
	It's just old stuff I'll be getting rid of it.

ANNIE turns the tap on. High pressure.

Hot.

RUKHSANA runs her hand under.

RUKHSANA	Very hot!
ANNIE	Bet you didn't have hot water where you was from?
DANNY	There was
RUKHSANA	In some places.
DANNY	In most places.
RUKHSANA	I'm looking forward to a bath!

ANNIE jams the tap off.

I always liked a good English bath!

ANNIE	Do you speak Indian, then, Danny?
RUKHSANA	Not much
ANNIE	Did you not teach him it?
RUKHSANA	Everyone spoke English.
ANNIE	That's funny coz the Indians in Forest Gate, they don't speak it.
	I never understood why Simon took off in the first place. Globetrotting.
	Fine. It's different. It's hot. Or it's cold. New food. New drink.
	But I coulda told you something shit like this would happen.
	I coulda told you that for nothing.
	Most of the time we don't even know what country you're in.
	Mum's on her deathbed, I can't reach him for weeks.

15

(*To* DANNY.)
Did you even know your dad had a sister?

(*To* RUKHSANA.)
Did *you* cut Danny off from *your* family as well?

Did you take him to see *them*?

(*Realising*.) Oh . . .
You didn't, did you?

What did you think about that, Danny?

I mean I couldn't understand it. This was my brother.
My nephew and I never see him. That's not right,
    is it?
What a bastard he was.

RUKHSANA   You made your views plain

ANNIE   You weren't there.

RUKHSANA   What you stood for.

ANNIE   You weren't there what was *so wrong* with
            what I stood for?
        No tell me
        What was so wrong? I was his sister, he didn't
            have to hate me!
        We would call him up at university he'd change
            his voice, pretend he was someone else.
        He was a bastard.

DANNY   Get lost.

ANNIE   (*To* RUKHSANA.)
        You got a right little Mogul here, don'tcha?

        Simon, he come to see Mum once in fifteen years.
        He don't even come back for the funeral.
        Oh he was a triffic son, he was a wonderful son
            f'r 'er.
        Still, Mum gives him the house.
        'He was better than us,' that's what she said
        'He went off to make the world a better place.'
        If you was better than us, why the fuck should you
            wanna come back?
        What can we offer you?

        You gonna be claiming?
        Is that why?
        I would, in your position.

Coz I bet he didn't leave you much. Did he? What
  did he leave ya?

Still you gotta look after your own, don't you?

She tosses RUKHSANA *the key.*

I contacted a school.
Well somebody had to.
In this country it's the law to go to school.
It's not too rough.

DANNY   We won't be here long.

ANNIE   Oh won'tcha?

RUKHSANA   No, we won't be here long at all

DANNY   We know where we're not welcome

ANNIE   I didn't say that. Did I?

             ANNIE *points to a plastic shopping bag.*

             I got some groceries.
             Happy Shopper
             It's round the corner.
             Patel's.
             (*Defensively.*) Nice people, you know? I didn't
               have a problem.
             I try to help you
             Do my duty
             Would you say I haven't tried to help you here?

RUKHSANA   He's dead.

             Beat. ANNIE *picks up her helmet, gently.*

ANNIE   Yeah.
             Yeah, I know.

             Goodbye, Danny.
             You got my number.
             You give me a call, yeah? If she can't hack it.

             DANNY *is silent.* ANNIE *exits.*

DANNY   I should have smacked her the way she spoke to
               you.

RUKHSANA   Yes!

DANNY   A right hook

RUKHSANA   In the teeth

DANNY   Put your dukes up, lady!

17

RUKHSANA	Ha!
	Something shifts in RUKHSANA. *A downturn.*
	Oh God.
DANNY	Sit down. It's OK. Go on.
	I'll make us a cup of tea
RUKHSANA	No
DANNY	Oh Mum
RUKHSANA	No tea
DANNY	Mum
RUKHSANA	It's nothing.
DANNY	You were doing really well today.
	(*Imitating* ANNIE.) 'I'll tell ya something for naffing'
RUKHSANA	Ha!
DANNY	'Do you speak Indian then, Danny?'
RUKHSANA	No comedy show!
DANNY	'I'll tell you something for nothing'
RUKHSANA	Your voices!
DANNY	'I'm telling ya, he was a bastard.'
RUKHSANA	Language
DANNY	Dad wasn't a bit like her, was he?
RUKHSANA	No
DANNY	When you first met him?
RUKHSANA	No
DANNY	Why did we not hear about her?
RUKHSANA	She made her views plain.
DANNY	And your parents?
	Why did we come back?
RUKHSANA	You always wanted to come back! You remember in India The hassling dirty boys Running alongside you, asking you
DANNY	(*In an Indian accent.*) 'What country?'

RUKHSANA 'What country?'

DANNY England!

RUKHSANA 'Englan!'

DANNY Englan!

RUKHSANA Manchester United!

DANNY *West Ham* United!

RUKHSANA Gary Lineker!

DANNY Why *did* we come here?

        Beat.

RUKHSANA Because you educate your children in England.
To do otherwise would sabotage your future.
Everyone knows that in the end you head to
    England.

DANNY I don't think this is what they meant.

RUKHSANA You remember that time in Bombay.
That awful hotel.
Before we found our apartment.
You turned the tap and it ran red.

DANNY The pipes were rusty.

RUKHSANA You thought it was blood.

DANNY I know now. The pipes were rusty.

RUKHSANA Remember how scared you were.
But this is England.

        Here we don't have to worry about anything.
Things not working or malaria pills or power cuts

DANNY Or roads

RUKHSANA Danny *please*

DANNY There aren't any roads in England

RUKHSANA *Please.*

DANNY This isn't what he said it was like

RUKHSANA I KNOW THIS ISN'T WHAT HE SAID.

        Beat.

DANNY All this stuff. Here. There must be something
    interesting.

RUKHSANA Don't

DANNY	Years and years old
RUKHSANA	Don't open it
DANNY	And not just . . . Grandma's
RUKHSANA	Danny!

DANNY opens up the trunk.

You don't know what you'll find.
Please

*DANNY pulls out, slowly, a motorcyclist's helmet.
A motorcyclist's jacket.*

*RUKHSANA is sick in the basin. DANNY is
forced to hold her.*

It must be the flight

DANNY	(*Sympathetic again.*) Yeah.
RUKHSANA	Just not used to / it.
DANNY	Yes.
RUKHSANA	I'm / OK
DANNY	You you sit down.

She sits down.

I'll clean you up.

RUKHSANA	Don't creep / around me, Danny!
DANNY	What?
RUKHSANA	I'm fine.
DANNY	(*Of the suit.*) It's probably Annie's. An old suit of Annie's.

She gazes at the motorcyclist's suit.

RUKHSANA	Yes

*She moves to it. She holds it. She barely listens
to DANNY.*

DANNY	Tomorrow. We'll start looking for somewhere else. We'll sell this place. Move further in. Mum? It's going to be great. Tomorrow, we'll get the newspapers. The *London Times*.

The *Manchester Guardian*.
Start looking for a job.
We'll make up your CV:
University of Sheffield, BA.

Mum?

Marketing manager.
High-level.
International.
A big glass office.
When India went international.

Tomorrow. Do you promise me?

You've been like this for weeks
But we're here now.
No more waiting.
You promised everything would be transformed.
As soon as we got here.
Are you listening to me?

Beat.

RUKHSANA   Will you leave me for a little bit?

Please. Go out. Explore the territory.

DANNY   You promised you were going to try

RUKHSANA   Yes. Tomorrow. Yes.

She doesn't kiss him.

DANNY *exits.* RUKHSANA *watches him leave, goes over to the bike helmet and stares it in the eye. She holds the suit.*

It's you, isn't it?
It's you.

You bastard
You won't even show your face.

You never said you had a motorbike before you met me.

There is no reply. She examines the jacket, which has little round subversive badges on it.

These little badges.
Southend. 1977.

You never told me, any of this!

She flings the helmet back into the trunk.

Did I ever know you?

She flings the suit back in the trunk. Shuts it.

She tries to exit, but the dimmer switch is at her eyeline. She stops. She lovingly reduces the light. Until it's all off.

Scene Four

The Pink Room

Later that evening. A master bedroom full of soft pink light and sleep. Hanging from the ceiling is an open clothes rack packed to bursting with women's clothes. To one side, a lady's dresser, packed with cosmetics.

LEON *speaks to the audience.*

LEON   Pretend

               He smears dark foundation on his face.

               There's no harm in this
               You like the feel of it.

               So let them go out, the old boy, the old gel
               Let them patch things up again
               And creep upstairs when the door slams.
               Scan the master bedroom.

               He did this place up for her
               New curtains
               Bamboo bedposts
               Winnie-the-Pooh footrug.
               'When he did that room up,' she says, 'I fell in
                   love wiv him all over again.'

               He takes his shirt off.

               So just pretend
               You've got all your life ahead of you
               All of the future.
               Choices.
               You could fall in love
               You could have kids
               You could earn a million.
               You could work in a car factory all yer life, there's
                   all to play for.

               He applies eyeliner in an impressionist style.

               There's no harm. There's no trouble. It's alright.

He opens one of his mother's dresser drawers.

The soft of lacies
Just try em on, for size, like, and *don't worry.*

Underwear falls from the sky into this room.

A lace slip descends from the ceiling. LEON
awaits it.

Blackout. Time briefly passes, then . . .

LEON *is wearing the slip, and* ROB, *holding*
LEON's *collar, has just swept* LEON's *face,*
smeared in mud pack, across the dresser. LEON
has also wet himself, although this isn't clear to
ROB *yet, partly because* LEON *disguises it. Both*
ROB, *and* LEON's *mum,* KAREN, *are somewhat*
undressed. KAREN *was wearing the dress that*
ROB *bought for her a few scenes ago.* ROB *has*
his shirt undone.

LEON	Aaaahhhh
ROB	Fackin
LEON	(And they think there's nobody home and they go for it)
ROB	Fackin
LEON	(And it just streams out)
ROB	Want me to put yer face to bed, do ya?
LEON	(Warm and I can't control it.)
ROB	Are you a girl?
LEON	No!
ROB	Putting your face on for a night on the town?
KAREN	ROB!
ROB	There are many things my son could have been There are many things my *son*
KAREN	LEEEVE him
LEON	(And I can see your argument, Dad, in all its clarity and you've got some rock-hard good points in there and I respect that I respect that, Dad)

KAREN	LEEEEVE him, Robert.
LEON	(And though my soul is flingin round the tumble-dryer)
ROB	It's not fuckin right, Kazza.
KAREN	It's
ROB	Not bleedin
KAREN	It's alright
ROB	We know he's a prat. We know he's a fuckin disaster zone. And now it turns out
KAREN	It's
ROB	He's a fackin queer.
KAREN	It's alright!
LEON	Not a queer!
ROB	Are you sayin that's alright, Karen?
LEON	No, it's not alright It wouldn't be.
	Mum, it's not fucking alright, is it?
ROB	Looks like an Asian Boy-George poofta.
	This is who we saved up for, Karen This is who we moved out for. This is our facking son. Disrespecting your beautiful things
KAREN	You're angry, Rob. I can see that.
	Yeah, course he is.
	Leave him to me, lover.
ROB	I just don't understand it
KAREN	I don't blame you, precious
ROB	I don't want him going wrong, that's all
KAREN	We're havin a hard time.
	He needs a woman's touch, Rob.
ROB	I'd say he's already had that!
LEON	No. Dad
	ROB *notices* LEON's *wet patch.*

24

ROB	Oh God, will you look at him?
KAREN	What?
ROB	He's only gone and

LEON *scrambles to cover himself up.*

	I do not believe it.
KAREN	What?
ROB	He's
KAREN	Oh
	Leave him to me, Rob.
ROB	It was gonna be a good night.
KAREN	It was a good night.
ROB	Yeah?
KAREN	So don't spoil it then.
	Off you go.

ROB *exits.*

	Oh it's alright, sweetheart.
	Why you goin putting on my things?
	Funny bunny.
	So which one's ya favourite?
LEON	What?
KAREN	Couldn't resist it. (*The joke.*)
	Ah, you've got it all smudged! (*The make-up.*)
LEON	Ah, shut up, Mum.
KAREN	You look very cosmopolitan.
	Thank God we noticed you in time, ay?
LEON	Fuck this for a laugh.

He makes to go.

KAREN	No, don't leave me, babe.
	Come back.
	I don't know what to do, Lee.

He comes back.

	Don't leave me.
LEON	I'm not
KAREN	Come here. Give us a cuddle.

He does.

You're alright.
You don't need to worry bout being a bit

She whistles.

These days.
This is 1995
You can be whoever you wanna be.

LEON   I *don't*.

KAREN   I reckon there's nuffin to be ashamed about.

LEON   I ain't.

KAREN   Fings are difficult between yer dad and me, Lee.
          Fings ain't right.
          Look at this (*The dress*.) he bought for me
            birthday.
          It's nice, ay?

Beat.

LEON   You gonna stay?

KAREN   Course I'll stay, darlin.
          I ain't leaving you.

          I promise.

Scene Five

Chips

The railings by the Dolphin, overlooking Romford Market.
DANNY *enters*.

DANNY   Hey, Dad
          I've caught the smell of it.
          Of England in the rain.
          The English countryside.
          It's distant but it's here.
          And when we struck that deal.
          For the one holiday we ever had here.
          You got nature.
          Hills
          Chalk formations
          Forests
          Limestone caves.
          And I got football and fish and chips.
          So we're on some country road

And stop off at a village
Some place with a green
And have a kickabout.
And do commentaries
In the voice of Kenneth Wolstenholme.
Do stupid voices from black-and-white comedy.

(*In a Pathé news accent.*)
'Put your dukes up, sonny,'
Charge me to the ground.
'You're asking for a bunch of fives,'
And I've ruined my jeans, and you don't care.
But Mum's angry.
So we get sent off to buy our national dish
Fish and chips
Vinegar steaming
Park bench soggy
Used to love that.
So she sends me off now, just like old times.
Fish and chips
Like it'll make it all worth it.
And I know
I'll end up with both portions.

DANNY *exits to obtain chips*.

STEVEN *and* LEON *enter.* STEVEN *is in the middle of some philosophising*.

STEVEN	I reckon she can take it or leave it I mean, granted There'll always be a small no-go period in any relationship.
LEON	That's right.
STEVEN	But there comes a time I mean I told her, 'I *want* to wait.' I tell her, 'I love you, Amy You know I respect ya Committed to ya' What you looking so miserable, Lee?
LEON	I ain't, mate – pleased for / ya.
STEVEN	Obviously, there are steps on the proverbial ladder.
LEON	What's that then?
STEVEN	I mean there are small vict'ries. One day you kiss her.

	One day you accidentally touch her bra. And once you're that far – (*Noticing* LEON's *glumness.*) WHAT?
LEON	Nah fair play to ya
STEVEN	And one day, once you're that far You say 'Amy – what do *you* think? *I* think it's time we took our relationship to a *deeper* level?'
LEON	'Would you like to make love?'
STEVEN	Fuck off 'make love'.
LEON	You said you loved her!
STEVEN	Yeah?
LEON	Did you mean it?
	Beat. STEVEN *remembers something.*
STEVEN	If you ever tell her, I swear.
LEON	What?
STEVEN	If that's what you're getting at
LEON	Oh no – in the past, mate, in the past. That was We were slaughtered and that was nothing anyway and anyway it was an accident. And anyway you gotta try everything once.
STEVEN	(*Breaking in.*) You what?
LEON	Nah, not everything! Point taken. I'm gonna do Jenny Tyler, aren't I?
STEVEN	Oh yeah?
LEON	Yeah.
STEVEN	You reckon?
LEON	If she'll have me.
	LEON *spots a car to change the subject.*
	Look at that That's criminal. Fuckin Datsun Datsun Sunny. Fuckin crap.
STEVEN	That's a Skoda.

LEON	It's a Datsun. I know my cars.
STEVEN	You ain't got a fuckin clue, mate. You ain't got much of a clue bout nothing, actually.
LEON	Genus 2.1, you can tell by the hubcaps
STEVEN	Hubcaps my arse, it's a fuckin Skoda.
	End of.
	I can't wait till I get me motor. Here y'are – have a look at these
	He takes out a bunch of keys
	Spare keys to the Cortina. Me dad's getting the Mondeo, innee? Metallic paint. Power steering Well, that's if it all don't fall apart. Things are touch and go, they say.
LEON	Oh no. It's sorted. I swear.
STEVEN	They won't get rid of the Asians. That's what my dad says.
LEON	They ain't laying nobody off.
STEVEN	Political correctness.
LEON	What's that then?
STEVEN	Speed humps in the brain.
LEON	My dad *told em*. Them upstairs. He fuckin He fuckin kicked them up the arse, mate.
STEVEN	The Cortina's mine when I pass me test. Pass me test first time, I will. Me dad's taking me down Rainham at Christmas. It's really quiet down there. He's gonna show me how to get the bite. I reckon I'll be alright at driving. I'll do the circuit. Steve-mobile bombing it round Romford Amy givin it (*He mimes fellatio.*)
LEON	You're fifteen
STEVEN	So?
LEON	You got two years, mate.
STEVEN	Yeah?
LEON	I might get a moped next birthday . . .

29

STEVEN	Yeah?
	LEON has forgotten that he is richer.
LEON	You coming out tonight?
STEVEN	Nah, mate Amy.
	LEON's glum again.
	WHAT IS IT?
LEON	What did I do?
STEVEN	Moping around.
LEON	Well, there's fuck all to do on me own, int there?
STEVEN	You should get a girl then. Or boy.
LEON	Fuck off.
STEVEN	Stay in then. Watch TV like normal people Course – you're not allowed to stay in, are ya? You'll start putting ya fingers in plug sockets.
LEON	No
STEVEN	Havin little accidents, burnin teatowels, pourin boilin water on yer arms.
LEON	Fuck off.
STEVEN	Pissing on the floor.
LEON	I did not piss on the floor.
STEVEN	What was goin through your mind as all your piss pissed over that carpet?
LEON	Shut up.
STEVEN	I couldn't believe it.
LEON	Someone spiked my drink.
STEVEN	Oh yeah?
LEON	Wish I'd never told ya. Thought you'd find it funny.
STEVEN	I did find it funny.
	Beat. LEON kicks the air.
LEON	If my dad asks you where I was, say I was with you, yeah?

Beat.

STEVEN	I'll say we was at the pictures. *Braveheart.*
LEON	Yeah . . . say that . . .

Thunder.

STEVEN	Ar, bollocks It don't never stop raining
LEON	That's Romford, though. Old, this market. Smell of it. It's old. Cobbles. It's good. Do you ever get that, Steve? This wacko fuckin feeling something's gone on here? In this marketplace, you know? You know Like the Battle of Agincourt?
STEVEN	What?
LEON	The Battle of Hastings Some big fuck-off historical The Battle of Waterloo. Could of done. Just sayin.
STEVEN	You're such a bender, Leon.
LEON	Leave it fuckin out, Steve.

Thunder and lightning. DANNY *enters with a
bags of chips, defiant at the sky.*

DANNY	Hey, bastard! Listen to me. I've caught the smell of it The countryside you said you missed. It's somewhere here. But is this what you always talked about?
LEON	(*To* STEVEN.) Fuck off is all I'm sayin, I ain't no fuckin I swear, Steve Please
DANNY	When you promised

LEON *spots* DANNY.

LEON	Oi!
DANNY	'We'll come back one day.'
STEVEN	Are you deaf?
DANNY	'We'll come home one day.'
	DANNY *faces them.*
LEON	Is it alright if I ponce a chip, mate?
	Is it alright if I ponce a chip, mate?
	What you so scared of? I only want a fuckin chip.
STEVEN	(*An 'Indian' accent.*) 'You speak English?'
DANNY	Have one.
	He unravels the packet. LEON *takes a chip.*
LEON	Did you think I was gonna hit you?
DANNY	No.
LEON	Yeah, well I might have done.
STEVEN	Where you from, then?
	Pause.
DANNY	London.
STEVEN	Where?
DANNY	Here.
LEON	London ain't here.
DANNY	(*To* STEVEN, *of a chip.*) You can have one too if you want.
STEVEN	Don't want a chip, mate.
DANNY	Sorry?
STEVEN	What you saying sorry for?
DANNY	What, mate?
STEVEN	What you saying 'mate' for, I ain't your mate?
	And I don't like Paki smelly Arab curry shit on top of chips.
	Greasy stink, like.
DANNY	Just salt and vinegar.
STEVEN	What's wrong with you?
	A glance at DANNY's *outfit.*

	Hi-Tecs, trousers with creases, where did you get this shit?

Hi-Tecs, trousers with creases, where did you get
  this shit?

And you're posh

LEON He ain't half posh.

STEVEN He is marbles-in-his-mouth posh.
Still
(*In a posh voice.*) 'Pleased to meet you.'

DANNY Yeah, pleased to meet you.

STEVEN (*In a posh voice.*) 'I'd like to shake you by the
  hand'

LEON *creases up.*

DANNY Yeah?

STEVEN Yeah.

STEVEN *reaches out his hand to shake* DANNY*'s
hand.* DANNY *moves to reciprocate, but at the
moment of contact* STEVEN *flashes it up instead,
smoothing his hair.*

Aaaaaaaaah.

Beat.

LEON Where are you from then?

DANNY England.

STEVEN *semi-lunges, not making or intending to
make contact.* DANNY *is frightened.*

STEVEN You ought to watch yourself. England! Who d'you
  think you are?
I mean – take it from me

LEON Go on, mate
Say something posh.

DANNY Get lost.

LEON Ha ha!
'Get lost'
Go on, say something else!
I like that, y'know? Posh voices.

STEVEN What?

DANNY What do you want me to say?

LEON Anything, mate.

STEVEN	Nonce.
DANNY	I can do, er
LEON	Don't matter what, mate.
STEVEN	He's winding me up now.
DANNY	'Put your dukes up, sonny'
STEVEN	What?
DANNY	'You're asking for a bunch of fives.'
	'Haven't you ever heard, never hit a man with spectacles.'
	STEVEN wallops DANNY in the stomach, then himself doubles up in pain.
STEVEN	Owwww
DANNY	What was that for?
STEVEN	Owww. Fuck. Fuckin hurt me hand.
DANNY	What did you bloody do that for?
STEVEN	Hit him, Lee. Go on. Hit 'im.
	LEON thinks, then gets DANNY, even harder, in the face, knocking him to the floor. DANNY's been really hurt. His eye is kind of bleeding.
	Come on, Lee.
	STEVEN exits.
	LEON bends down.
LEON	I didn't mean to do that. I didn't mean to hit so hard and Jesus you're bleeding.
	He touches DANNY's cheek, but DANNY whips it away.
	Sorry!
	Poor fucking thing with shit clothes!
	Listen Mate You wanna come over to mine?
DANNY	What? No!

34

| LEON | Get it cleared up? |
| | It's close. |

Beat. STEVEN *reappears.*

STEVEN	Leon, you bender!
LEON	I just needed to hit something.
	That's all.

DANNY *gets up, faces* LEON, *and exits.*
STEVEN *exits in the opposite direction.* LEON
speaks to DANNY's *disappearing figure.*

So listen, the bruises don't last long.
And the cuts close up.
I should know coz I've had em.
I'm really sorry
But you don't wanna walk around with an eye
   like that.
So now it's done
This is what you have to do:
Sweep indoors without no one seeing
Lock yourself in the loo
And what you need is some foundation.
Your mum should have some.
Match it to the colour of your skin.
You should cake it on, too
And if you can't find that
Then Clearasil will do.

Scene Six

The Motorcyclist

RUKHSANA's *house.* RUKHSANA, *by the trunk. Out of which
she pulls the motorcyclist's leathers, and hangs them, man-shaped,
on a rack. She finds the helmet, placing it on top, for a head. She
gazes at it.*

*She continues to search in the trunk. She pulls out a little tin of
tobacco. She registers it.*

| RUKHSANA | For your roll-ups |

*She opens it. Some ancient rolling papers and the
rest – she blows – is dust.*

Gone to dust
But I could smell it on your breath when you took
   it up again

> The shock of not knowing you
> The smell on your breath
> And when you bought that bike
> It was me who felt betrayed.
>
> I can explain everything. As you rode across the
>   city I was prepared to
> Tell you everything.
> But how can I now?

The phone rings. She freezes. It continues to ring.

> I won't pick up the phone till
> Till we
> Get this straight . . .

The phone stops ringing. It goes to answerphone.

DANNY comes out of his bedroom, wearing a white school shirt, blazer and trousers. He is listening to his Walkman.

DANNY You didn't pick up the phone?

He checks the machine.

There's a message

RUKHSANA What's on the Walkman?

DANNY Tapes.

RUKHSANA What's on them?

DANNY Hindi language.

RUKHSANA In Bombay you could have had lessons.

DANNY You didn't seem fussed.

RUKHSANA I could have taught you.

DANNY You were busy.

DANNY plays the message. It is, coincidentally, KAREN.

KAREN Y'hello, Mrs Parrish? My name's Karen. I'm calling from Anderson Leigh – you applied for a position with us, the Marketing Officer? Yeah, I'm just calling to say we'd like to meet you to talk about the position and any questions you might have? Congratulations! I'm Mr Leigh's PA, so perhaps you could give me a call about arranging an interview at our city office? 0171 287 4141. / Alright? OK, bye!

RUKHSANA	I haven't applied for any jobs
DANNY	No you haven't.
RUKHSANA	Did / you
DANNY	You did a job like this in India.
RUKHSANA	In *India*, / yes
DANNY	You didn't stop going on about it, drove us all crazy. Everything you said though
RUKHSANA	Did you *make an application?*
DANNY	I made you out really good! I said you were in the thick of it. When India went international. When all the phones started ringing. All those words. Glass offices. Corporate functions. Conferences. Solutions. The twenty-first century.
RUKHSANA	What if I had picked up the phone?
DANNY	I would have done your voice.
RUKHSANA	You can't do my voice.
DANNY	I fooled your secretary.
RUKHSANA	Since then your voice has broken fast.
	Beat.
DANNY	You promised you were going to try.
RUKHSANA	You tried on your school uniform.
DANNY	So you change the subject?
RUKHSANA	Let's have a look.
	She tries to arrange the school tie around his neck.
	I'll show you how to do the knot.
DANNY	I can do the knot.
RUKHSANA	I think it's a good school.
DANNY	You haven't seen it.
RUKHSANA	I read the booklet.
DANNY	I've seen it. It's a giant piece of concrete. All the boys have their heads shaved. Like the whole school's been infected with lice. You said I had to come back here for my *education*.

37

It's no good, Mum – all this stuff – all these
curtains closed – how's that gonna help?

RUKHSANA You'll make friends.

DANNY It's not about friends

RUKHSANA And all the girls will be after you.

DANNY Fuck off

RUKHSANA Language

DANNY Fuck off

RUKHSANA Just look at you.

DANNY I mean it.

RUKHSANA So handsome.

She spots something.

What's on your face?

DANNY Nothing.

RUKHSANA Make-up?

DANNY No.

RUKHSANA It looks like foundation.

DANNY No!

RUKHSANA What is it?

DANNY It's nothing.

RUKHSANA Let's see.

DANNY It's for spots.

RUKHSANA It'll give you spots.
Let me

She tries to wipe DANNY's face.

DANNY Get off.

RUKHSANA Daniel.

DANNY Don't touch me!

She tries to wipe his face harder.

Aaahwwwh!

The bruising is revealed. Pause.

RUKHSANA What happened?

DANNY Fell over.

RUKHSANA	No.
DANNY	Tripped on my laces.
RUKHSANA	Someone hit you.
DANNY	No.
RUKHSANA	Why didn't you tell me?
DANNY	What could you have done? Don't touch me No, seriously.
	I don't even know you care.
	So what, it's all his old stuff, (*On the floor.*) so what? You were getting divorced, anyway.
RUKHSANA	Not divorced
DANNY	Separated, whatever.
	I know why, as well. Your disappearances. Did you have an affair?
RUKHSANA	I'm going out
DANNY	Did you?
RUKHSANA	No.
DANNY	Go out then. If you're going to go out.
RUKHSANA	I'll sort it out
DANNY	Don't come back until you do.
RUKHSANA	Don't say that.
DANNY	Don't come back until you do.

DANNY angrily collects the things on the floor and puts them back in the trunk. But he spots something in there. A shoebox. He opens it. A shoebox full of tapes. He looks at them. Picks one out. Puts it in his Walkman. It plays loud in his head.

It is a scratchy recording of a radio comedy from, say, 1956 – a cross perhaps between Hancock's Half Hour *and* Steptoe and Son. *The show features* STEVE POTTS, *an Estuary electrician with ideas and aspirations above his station; his vulgar sister* WINNIE POTTS, *and* PROFESSOR

> HULLABALOO, *an expert in the Hindoostanee*
> *tongue. Gags are followed by extravagant,*
> *prolonged laughter from the studio audience.*
> *The tape is halfway through.*
>
> DANNY *sits. He listens. He is bathed in this.*
>
> *Laughter.*

STEVE POTTS

> Oh Winnie, I never seen a more beauteous sight,
> I tell you I nearly fell off me ladder

WINNIE POTTS

> So what did she look like?

STEVE POTTS

> I couldn't ascertain that.

WINNIE POTTS

> What d'you mean?

STEVE POTTS

> She wore a crimson veil to disguise her aspect

WINNIE POTTS

> Oh you do pick em, don'tcha?
>
> *Laughter.*
>
> How do you know she ain't mutton dressed as
> lamb?

STEVE POTTS

> Oh but Winnie, we're in love!

WINNIE POTTS

> Any old sheep could stick a tea towel on her head
> and pretend she's the Queen of Bombay.

STEVE POTTS

> Cherrypondi

WINNIE POTTS

> Eh?

STEVE POTTS

> She's from Cherrypondi

WINNIE POTTS

> Cherry Brandy?

STEVE POTTS

> Don't mind if I do.

Huge laughter.

At least I think that was where she was from.
Her English weren't awfully good.

WINNIE POTTS

I wouldn't mind being an Indian princess, myself –
do you think she'd want me along as lady in
waiting?

STEVE POTTS

I'm afraid her manners are far too refined for you,
Winnie.

WINNIE POTTS

Oh very nice, your own sister.

STEVE POTTS

No, I don't think you'd fit in at all.

WINNIE POTTS

Well, what do you think the Maharajah's gonna
make of an electrician from Barking marrying
his daughter?

STEVE POTTS

He won't find out

WINNIE POTTS

Eh?

STEVE POTTS

I intend to disguise myself as a Hindoostanee prince.

Laughter.

Have a look at this.

The audience scream with hilarity, as STEVEN
POTTS *whips out . . .*

WINNIE POTTS

Oh my lawd.

STEVE POTTS

A Hindoostanee turban! I got it in the docks at a
knock-down price from some seamen from East
Pakistan.

WINNIE POTTS

How knock-down?

STEVE POTTS

I said I'd knock em down if they didn't hand it
over!

WINNIE POTTS

    Quite right.

    But you don't speak a word of Hindoostanee, Steven.

STEVE POTTS

    Don't you worry, Winnie, don't you worry.

    Segway sitar music, which occasions laughter and clapping. The rattling of tea cups and saucers.

    Professor Hullaballoo, it's terribly kind of you to teach me the Hindoostanee tongue at such short notice.

    Laughter.

    He may be an expert in the Hindoostanee tongue, but PROFESSOR HULLABALLOO's *English has a quite extraordinary accent.*

PROFESSOR HULLABALLOO

    My son, I am only delighted to have such an eager student of our humble language.

STEVE POTTS

    Ask me anything, Professor Hullaballoo. Put me to the test.

PROFESSOR HULLABALLOO

    Very well. Repeat after me, and try to make your pronunciation sound like mine.

    The phrase meaning 'Do you understand English?' – '*Kyaa aap Angrezee samazhteehey?*'

STEVE POTTS

    Kyaa aap Angrezee samazhteehey?

PROFESSOR HULLABALLOO (*Corrects his response.*)

    '*Angrezee*'

STEVE POTTS

    Angrezee

PROFESSOR HULLABALLOO

    Excellent!

    '*Samazhteehey*'

STEVE POTTS

    Samazhteehey

PROFESSOR HULLABALLOO

    Ohhhhh jolly golly good! '*Kyaa aap Angrezee samazhteehey?*' – 'Do you speak English?' Now

you have learned everything you will ever need
to know!

But tell me my son, why do you desire to learn our
humble tongue?

*Pause. And outside the radio programme something
odd happens. A flicker somewhere. Something
magic. DANNY notices something, but he doesn't
know what.*

STEVE POTTS

Well, Professor, it's because I've fallen madly
in love.
Completely.
Utterly in love.
So deeply I may never ever escape.

Scene Seven

Strip of Green

The strip of green, sunset.

ANNIE *enters in clothes for farming. Wellingtons. She is planting
a rose bush.*

RUKHSANA *enters.* ANNIE *doesn't recognise her.*

ANNIE   Oi
             Can't you read?
             This is private property

             Do you understand English?

RUKHSANA   Yes.
             I can understand English.

ANNIE   Oh . . .

RUKHSANA   You said I could find you here.

ANNIE   I don't own it.
             The farmer employs me.

             We're trying to get the planting done before the
                 frost gets bad.
             He's started a sideline in roses.
             You
             You gotta give em time to take root
             Before they're under pressure to flower.

RUKHSANA   What's the fire over there?

43

ANNIE	Dead wood.
RUKHSANA	I like it here. It's like countryside.
ANNIE	Horses down there.
RUKHSANA	The concrete starts again soon enough.

Beat.

ANNIE	You left Danny on his own, did you?
RUKHSANA	Yes.
ANNIE	Well, you can't stay here long.

The farmer will come and get you with his gun!

Beat. That was a joke. RUKHSANA *stares at* ANNIE.

You doing anything nice for Christmas?

RUKHSANA	No. You?

Beat. ANNIE *shrugs.*

You not spending it with your . . .

ANNIE	Bill? Hah! No, I ain't spending it with Bill.

Pause.

He fucked off, didn't he? Years ago.
That's an old story.

I wanted to have kids and he didn't.
Then coupla years ago he goes all daft – some
    mid-life crisis and all of a sudden he thinks he
    wants to procreate.
But after all that it turns out I can't have em
    anyway and so he fucks off.
I think, suit yerself, but by then I'm forty.
Wouldn't want him as a father anyway.

Nah, you're better off without them, aren't you?
You're better off.

RUKHSANA	What was he like? Simon. When you knew him?
ANNIE	Oh no.
RUKHSANA	What was he like?
ANNIE	I ain't doing this.

RUKHSANA	In that house there are All these things In boxes.
ANNIE	You looked?
RUKHSANA	Can't help it.
ANNIE	Stupid
RUKHSANA	Clothes. Things. A tin of tobacco.
ANNIE	Should have burned it all years ago.
RUKHSANA	But you left it.

ANNIE	Stuffed in boxes, never opened them!
	It wasn't worth opening to get to burning.
	I don't think he could make anyone happy in the
	   long term, Simon.
	All his *ideas* he dragged you into, the way he got
	   you so enthusiastic, then he just turns his back
	   and fucks off.
	At least you got Danny. Be grateful for that.

Pause. RUKHSANA *produces the tin of tobacco dust.* ANNIE *takes it.*

	We used to go down London on the bikes. Down the East End. And sometimes we went out into Essex. Used to go to these amazing pubs. He used to smoke these dirty little roll-ups. We used to go to gigs. Some bands we saw become famous. It was the happiest time of my life. And he was *funny*.
RUKHSANA	Yeah?
ANNIE	Really funny. He cracked me up.
RUKHSANA	He *was* funny. I had forgot that.
ANNIE	But when he fucked off to university it was like he became a different person. Everything changed. Tried to chuck all his old gear out.

ANNIE *gives the tin back.*

RUKHSANA	You know . . . he was on a motorbike . . . when he died?
ANNIE	No. No I didn't know that.

45

RUKHSANA	He'd just bought it
ANNIE	I didn't know that.
	Listen. Christmas Day. You and Danny could come round. I could cook.
	Beat.
RUKHSANA	Do you ever have blue sky in this country?
	Beat.
ANNIE	Well, fuck off then.
RUKHSANA	I'm sorry.
ANNIE	No, if you're gonna be like that you can fuck off.
	RUKHSANA *turns and heads off.*
	You're a disgrace, you know? Your poor son. Snap out of it. Forget about Simon.
	Forget about him. Before it's too late or you'll end up like me. Your mind will spin round and round You'll end up useless Working on a fucking farm. You'll age fifty years. You'll die.
	Did you hear me?
	Beat.

Scene Eight

Canary Wharf

Outside his house, ROB *is polishing the hubcaps of his car.*
LEON *appears.*

ROB *freezes.*

LEON	You want me to help you, Dad?
ROB	I don't want you to creep around me.
LEON	I'm not. I, I Mended that shelf.

	So
	All I'm saying is that's one thing off your list.
	Beat.
ROB	Cheers.
LEON	Freezin, innit? It's definitely . . . winter now.
	Pause. ROB *looks at Canary Wharf in the far distance.*
ROB	Can you see that, Leon?
	LEON *sees it.*
LEON	Yeah.
ROB	I've been watchin it. Coz when night falls, they're gonna turn on all the lights. They couldn't afford it until today – too much office space empty.
	The funny thing is, *we* can see *it*, but from up there they can't see *us*. Just a mess of houses. From up top Canary Wharf, you can't see where London ends and Romford begins.
	I told em I said, 'Granted, we're still in recession. But you can't chuck half of us just because the Deutschmark's falling and the boys in Frankfurt are willing to do something for nothing.' That took em by surprise. I said, 'I read the financial pages. I tape *The Money Programme*.'
LEON	They don't expect you to have something up there.
ROB	That's right. They don't expect that. Them upstairs. I told em, 'They're switching the lights on again aren't they? What does that tell ya? We're on the upturn.' I showed them the article I cut out.
LEON	What did they say?
ROB	They said, 'Thanks, we'll have a look at that.' They're gonna build more of em – these skyscrapers. There'll be a whole skyline. The greatest financial centre in the world. It'll beat New York. It'll beat Tokyo.

And it'll *cane* fucking Frankfurt.

I was born two minutes walk away from that. Your nan and grandad moved me away coz it wasn't a nice area . . . now it's gonna be the greatest business centre in the whole world.

And they laugh at me at reception. They're all Essex. But they try and make that they're something better.

I dint mean to shout so loud, Leon.

LEON	No – you were right.
ROB	It was The surprise of it, you know? Walkin in on ya.
LEON	You was right to be angry.
ROB	It's just
LEON	You were right, mate.
ROB	I er The motor was makin funny noises. I bet it's the carburettor. You seen how the carburettor works? I could show you. It's a tricky little thing.
LEON	You showed me before.
ROB	Oh, right / sorry
LEON	Nah you could show / me again
ROB	Don't be daft
LEON	It's a lovely motor.
ROB	I might have to sell it.
LEON	You won't
ROB	Sell the hubcaps, anyway. Jesus you didn't half look different with that gunk on . . . You are just messin around, intcha?
LEON	Course I'm I'm toughening myself up, Dad. I do press-ups.
ROB	I wondered what the creaking was

48

Pause.

I mean, it's a free country and all but
I wanna make sure you turn out right.
If you turned out . . . a bit
(*He whistles.*)
D'you understand me?
You are just messin around?

LEON   Course.

ROB   Yeah?

LEON   There are girls at school I like.

ROB   Yeah?

LEON   Yeah.

ROB   (*An assessment.*) Well, you're not too bad.

        Pause.

        You could invite one of them out for a date,
            couldn't you?

LEON   Dad!

ROB   Here y'are.

        He gets out his wallet and gives LEON *a fiver.*
        LEON *takes it, forlornly.*

        Christmas coming.

LEON   Yeah.

ROB   We could put the lights out at the weekend.
        Go up the loft
        Get the reindeers down.
        We'll have a good one this year, Lee.

Scene Nine

Speaking to Gravestones

That evening. RUKHSANA, *in the Docklands, staring at the
Canary Wharf Tower. Which is still mainly in darkness. She holds
the tobacco tin as if it were a tiny urn.*

RUKHSANA   Hey
            You.
            So people speak to gravestones, don't they?
            And I've been having trouble getting through.

And I think you'd have loved this.
You'd have loved to wire this whole building.
And I remember you took me here in 1977.
When all this was just mud and rusting metal.
You waved your arms about. Talked about the
    future
I can see you
Right here, waving your arms about.
Lamenting its darkness
Gazing at it
Like you'd invented veins.
You bastard, you never said a word about anything
    east of here.

But I will
Release you
If you believe me.
I loved you. I was faithful. I will explain everything.
Do you believe me?

*Beat. Then the lights of Canary Wharf flicker on,
slowly, magically. She gazes, amazed.*

Good.
Danny's waiting at home for me.
But he's going to have to wait

The tip of the tower flashes.

We have a lot to talk about.
Before I leave you.

Scene Ten

Unit One

*Morning. The comedy tape is playing as the scene begins.
DANNY is in the kitchen, wearing his school uniform. He is
making a packed lunch for his first day at school. He repeats some
of the words after the comedy tape.*

STEVE POTTS

    Professor Hullaballoo, it's terribly kind of you to
    teach me the Hindoostanee tongue at such short
    notice.

    Laughter.

DANNY   (*Imitating* STEVE POTTS.)
    'Professor Hullaballoo, it's terribly kind of you . . . '

PROFESSOR HULLABALLOO
My son, I am only delighted to have such an eager
student of our humble language.

STEVE POTTS
Ask me anything, Professor Hullaballoo. Put me
to the test.

PROFESSOR HULLABALLOO
Repeat after me, and try to make your pronunciation
sound like mine.

DANNY   Mum!

DANNY rips off his headphones furiously.

Where are you? You can't just not be here. *Mum.*

*Then, a piece of magic. Something happens inside
the motorcyclist. DANNY nearly misses it, but he
doesn't miss it. DANNY investigates.*

Nothing.

Mum!

*Another burst of magic. Spooked, DANNY puts
the headphones on again, as a method of returning
to sanity.*

STEVE POTTS
Ask me anything, Professor Hullaballoo. Put me
to the test.

PROFESSOR HULLABALLOO
Repeat after your father, and try and make your
pronunciation sound like his.

*And then DANNY's father is magically on the
tape.*

HIS DAD'S VOICE
Hello, Danny

DANNY rips off his headphones, spooked as hell.

*He puts them on again. The tape has moved on a
little bit . . .*

I dint touch nuffing

Beat.

DANNY   I dint touch nuffing

HIS DAD'S VOICE
Nuffing

51

DANNY   Nuffing

HIS DAD'S VOICE
                 Come on, Sunshine

DANNY   Come on, Sunshine

HIS DAD'S VOICE
                 We all got inta the Fiesta

DANNY   We all got inta the Fiesta

HIS DAD'S VOICE
                 And went Nan's for tea

DANNY   And went Nan's for tea

HIS DAD'S VOICE
                 Tea

DANNY   Tea

HIS DAD'S VOICE
                 Oh Danny

DANNY   Yeah?

HIS DAD'S VOICE
                 At the end of the day

DANNY   At the end of the day

                 And DANNY *is ready to go out now, gathers his*
                 stuff and leaves.

HIS DAD'S VOICE
                 We'll go back to Essex
                 But don't tell your mother.
                 Return to the land of my birth
                 It's not what you think, it's different
                 But I missed it. So much.
                 I missed the yellows in the summer
                 The burnt grasses
                 The hubcaps in the scrapyard
                 The hubcaps in the rosebeds.

                 There is sudden and intense snowfall, like a
                 swoon.

Scene Eleven

Snowfall

RUKHSANA *and* DANNY's *house. Afternoon.*

RUKHSANA *is wearing a business suit, looking outside.*

DANNY *enters, in school uniform.*

Pause.

RUKHSANA   Hello
Have you seen the snow?
It's astonishing!

You look cold.

We'll have to get you a proper coat!

DANNY *puts his bag down.*

So how was school?

How were the other kids?

Danny, come on, speak to me

Was it rough?

Was it racist?

Because, listen, we can find you another one.
    That's no problem.

I'm sorry I wasn't here last night.

DANNY   Really I don't care what you do.

RUKHSANA   There was something I had to do.

DANNY   Did he follow you over here?

Beat.

RUKHSANA   There was never anyone other than your father.

Beat.

DANNY   School
School was great.

Better than looking after you.

They were friendly

RUKHSANA   What did you say?

DANNY   'Alright'

RUKHSANA	What did they say?
DANNY	'Alright'
	Why are you wearing that? (*The suit*.)
RUKHSANA	I called that woman back. About the interview.
DANNY	Did you?
RUKHSANA	I can do that job
DANNY	Can you?
RUKHSANA	They're going to fit me in at the end of the day Will you come with me? You can help me. Mock interview. You can decide whether they're good enough. And afterwards We'll go into London. Have dinner. See some sights. We can decide where we want to move to.
DANNY	It's too late.
RUKHSANA	What?
DANNY	I mean I already have plans. Some people from school. Invited me out
RUKHSANA	Some friends?
DANNY	I don't know.
RUKHSANA	What are they called?
DANNY	Lewis. Tom. Amy.
RUKHSANA	Amy?
DANNY	Shut up.
RUKHSANA	Will there be alcohol?
DANNY	Shut up.
	Pause.
RUKHSANA	Please. Come with me. You can go out tomorrow Please.
DANNY	It's too late.

RUKHSANA	I forbid you
DANNY	You can't.
	It's too late.
	Pause.
RUKHSANA	I'll never disappear again, Danny.
	I'll be here when you get home.
	Danny.
	Well will you wish me luck?
	Please.
	Pause.

Scene Twelve

We're Going Out Tonight

ROB's *house, a little later that afternoon.* STEVEN *and* LEON *are still in school uniform, their ties at quarter-length.*

STEVEN	Just take some.
LEON	No.
STEVEN	I'll ask him, he likes me.
	He's sound, your dad.
LEON	He only lets me drink if he's around.
	He don't think we're old enough.
STEVEN	I'm old enough. I can hold my drink.
LEON	(*Affirmatively.*) Oh yeah.
STEVEN	We goin down the ditch tonight?
LEON	I thought you was going out with Amy?
STEVEN	Yeah, she was comin.
LEON	Too good for us, is she?
STEVEN	Oh fuck off, Leon.
	We're taking a break, int we?
LEON	Why?
STEVEN	I told her first!
	I say:
	'It's not working Amy.'
	You know what I mean?
LEON	Plenny more fish in the sea, though.

Beat.

STEVEN	More fun with the boys anyway.
LEON	Eh?
STEVEN	Nah. (*He doesn't mean anything by that.*)
LEON	It's good to have you back, mate.
STEVEN	We'll take some beers, like.
LEON	Get mashed up. Find some girls!
STEVEN	(*Explodes.*) I'll fucking do him if I see him.
LEON	Who?
STEVEN	Fuckin
LEON	Who?
STEVEN	It don't matter who, Leon.

Beat.

LEON	So where we gonna get the beers from?
STEVEN	Your dad
LEON	I told you
STEVEN	Off-licence, then.
LEON	We won't get served
STEVEN	I'll get served. 'Ere y'are – got some fags yesterday.
LEON	You'll get cancer.
STEVEN	I don't get cancer.

LEON *gasps in admiration.*

Enter ROB, *hassled.* STEVEN *frantically hides the cigarettes.*

Alright, Rob

ROB	Steven.
LEON	We're going out, Dad
ROB	Yeah?
LEON	With the lads like.
ROB	In the snow?
LEON	Not too cold.

ROB	Making snowmen, are you?
LEON	Is that alright, Dad?
	Beat.
ROB	Yeah.
STEVEN	Rob, yeah?
ROB	Listen, boys
STEVEN	How old would you say I was, Rob?
ROB	I know how old you are, Steven. You're in my son's class at school.
STEVEN	Yeah, but if you didn't know that, how old would you say I was? Fifteen, seventeen, eighteen?
ROB	Thirteen, I'd say
STEVEN	No, seriously

ROB	Your balls have barely dropped Steven.
	It's not so long I remember you in here bawling
	    your eyes out coz you grazed your knee on the
	    patio.
	
	You said your dad was gonna come round and beat
	    me up.

	STEVEN *clicks his neck.*
STEVEN	How's work, Rob? You was in London today weren'tcha?
LEON	Can me and Steve have a Heineken?
STEVEN	What's wrong, Rob?
ROB	You got the head for it, Steve?
STEVEN	What?
ROB	For a Heineken.
STEVEN	Course.
ROB	Yeah, you can have a Heineken.
LEON	Ah, it's beautiful, Heineken.
ROB	We'll see if you have the head for it.
LEON	Can we take a couple down the ditch and all?
ROB	Oh yeah?

STEVEN	Leon reckons he's in tonight.
ROB	Is that right, Lee? You takin a beer for a lady too, are ya?
LEON	Well, we'll see how it goes.
ROB	Good man.
LEON	If she'll have me.
	LEON *moves into the kitchen*.
ROB	Should be int'restin, anyway. You can get me one an all, Lee. (*Clarifying*.) A beer, not a little girl.
	LEON *goes out to get a beer*.
	Can fackin do with one . . .
STEVEN	Why's that?
ROB	You look after him, Steve.
STEVEN	Yeah, alright.
ROB	He's alright, isn't he?
STEVEN	My old boy said there were more meetings today.
ROB	I'm not in the mood.
STEVEN	Have you heard anything, though? I hear they're not going to lay off any of the Pakistanis Any of the blacks.
ROB	I wouldn't know.
STEVEN	He reckons you upstairs
ROB	I'm not upstairs.
STEVEN	The talk is that you upstairs wouldn't be sorry to take the package.
ROB	What does he know?
	ROB *remembers that he is, relatively, a little bit upstairs*.
	Sorry
STEVEN	He's got repayments to make, Rob. Christmas coming up
	LEON *shouts, from off*.
LEON	Oh shit

ROB	What you done now?
LEON	Oh shit oh shit oh shit
ROB	What?
LEON	I'm sorry, Dad.
	LEON *appears with the beers. He has spilt them all down him.*
	I'm really sorry.
ROB	What?
LEON	I've spilt it all down me.
ROB	You wally.
STEVEN	Seriously, Rob
ROB	(*To both, or either of them.*) I'm not going to hang you out to dry.
	He looks at both, separately. He walks off.
	The boys drink their beer. STEVEN *clicks his neck.*
STEVEN	You got any deodorant, Lee?
LEON	Yes, mate
STEVEN	Give us some? I left mine at home.
LEON	Lynx Africa?
STEVEN	Goo on then.
	LEON *tosses* STEVEN *the can. It looks like Lynx Africa, but it isn't.*
	What's this?
	'Menzone'. 'Menzone Musk'? What the fuck is Menzone?
LEON	I got it down the market.
STEVEN	It's fake.
LEON	Try it, it's alright.
	STEVEN *thinks. He opens his shirt up.*
	He sprays his armpit. Cautiously – as if dipping his toe in the sea.
STEVEN	Don't look, then.

59

LEON   Not looking.

                 STEVEN *sprays his armpit long enough to make*
                 some difference to the burgeoning rupture in the
                 ozone layer.

                 Yeah, easy on with it.

                 STEVEN *pointedly sprays for another five*
                 seconds, then gives the other armpit a deluge.

                 Oh come on, Steve

STEVEN   FUCK OFF, YOU QUEER

                 STEVEN *sprays it down his pants, then tosses*
                 LEON *the can.*

LEON   What's got into you?

STEVEN   Let me borrow your Ralph Lauren jumper, yeah?

                 Beat.

                 Do you want to go out or what?

LEON   Yeah, alright.

                 STEVEN *gets* LEON *in a headlock and sprays*
                 deodorant at him . . . and they play-fight . . .

                 . . . as DANNY *becomes part of the scene.*
                 DANNY *stands on his bed, listening to the tapes,*
                 doing the actions. The motorcyclist's kit is nearby.

HIS DAD'S VOICE
                 Stand with your legs apart, with a pint in one
                    hand, and make your point with the other.
                 Your elbows at right angles
                 You should never change that angle.

                 DANNY *plays with his new kinaesthetic.*

                 You drink at that angle

                 DANNY *drinks at that angle.*

                 You fight at that angle

                 DANNY *slings a punch.*

                 Click your neck and make conversation

                 DANNY *clicks his neck, and:*

DANNY   You
                 Alright, mate?

HIS DAD'S VOICE
            Not so bad, yerself?

DANNY   Not so bad, yerself?

HIS DAD'S VOICE
            Not so bad . . . how ya keeping?

            Pause.

DANNY   Goin down the Hammers soon

HIS DAD'S VOICE
            Oh yeah?

DANNY   Taking little Jason

HIS DAD'S VOICE
            Oh yeah?

            Well take care of yerself, mate

DANNY   Yeah, take care of yerself . . .
            Be good.

            DANNY *applies deodorant, excessively. He puts
            on the motorcyclist's leather jacket. It looks good.*

Scene Thirteen

The Docklands

RUKHSANA *is waiting in a glassy office, in her suit. A PA's desk,
a phone. A sofa. On a table rests an architect's model. A vision of
the Docklands in the future.* RUKHSANA *holds a glass of water.*
KAREN *emerges from another room – Mr Leigh's office.*

KAREN   He won't be long
            Are you sure you just want water?
            We just got ourselves a cappuccino machine.

RUKHSANA   I'm fine. Thank you.

KAREN   Seems a shame to just have water. Mr Leigh, he
               loves his coffee.
            And there's all sorts of variations.
            All sorts of things to sprinkle on top.
            He's always popping in just to try a new one –
               I don't get no work done!
            No need to be nervous.
            You'll be fine.

RUKHSANA   I like this. This model.

61

KAREN   That's how it's all gonna look. When it's finished.
              And it's where we're moving.
              Only a few more weeks here.
              We're moving to the Docklands.
              I'm being made office manager.
              I'll show you where we're going.

              She points to the place.

              There.
              A converted warehouse.
              It'll make the commute easier, anyway.
              You're Romford, aren't ya?

RUKHSANA   Yes.

KAREN   I remember from the letter!
              I put you on the top of the pile.
              I'm Romford, too, y'see.
              It's not too bad, is it?

RUKHSANA   No.

KAREN   It could be worse.
              Mr Leigh commutes from Surrey.
              He's got this massive house but it takes for ever.

              Your husband English, is he?

RUKHSANA   Yes.

KAREN   That's where you get the Parrish from?

RUKHSANA   Yes.

KAREN   I was gonna say
              Coz that's not an Indian name, is it?
              What's he do, then?

RUKHSANA   He's in construction.

KAREN   It's a good field to be in.

RUKHSANA   He plans the electrics. The wiring.
              For these big buildings.
              In big cities.
              He gets very taken up with it

KAREN   It's that kind of work.

RUKHSANA   And you wouldn't think you could
              Talk for so long about
              So many light bulbs.

KAREN   Boys and their toys, ay?

RUKHSANA	You get dragged in.
KAREN	You do.
RUKHSANA	If you're not careful.
KAREN	If you're not careful. That's right.
	They don't understand you working, do they? That's the thing.
	My husband he basically thinks I'm a typist but I'm so much more!
	'How was your day,' he goes, and before I can answer he goes:
	'Boring was it?'
	'No . . . Beg yer pardon but I love my job.'
	And if he doesn't appreciate that . . .
	Did you ever get that?
RUKHSANA	Yes
KAREN	Is that wrong?
	Beat.
RUKHSANA	Sometimes I thought it would be better just to take off. Forget him. Leave my son in his care and just take off.
	KAREN *thinks.*
	When you no longer reward each other.
	KAREN *thinks.*
	I left my husband. At last. Yesterday.
	It was the right thing to do.
	Pause. A buzzer on KAREN's *desk goes off.*
KAREN	That's you.
RUKHSANA	Right.
KAREN	Mr Leigh, he's a nice man.
RUKHSANA	Thank you.
KAREN	I hope you get it.
RUKHSANA	Thank you.
	KAREN *leads* RUKHSANA *into Mr Leigh's office. She returns. She thinks. She looks at her model, which glows, in the darkness, just like the real thing.*

Scene Fourteen

All the Dinner Parties

The master bedroom. KAREN *is updating her make-up.* ROB, *tired, enters, in his socks.* KAREN *notices. Outside there is a neon reindeer.*

KAREN	You scared me.
ROB	Got no shoes on.
KAREN	What you creeping up for?
ROB	Admiring ya.
KAREN	Well, don't, I'm not fit to be seen.
ROB	Oh, you are. You see Leon and Steve getting ready? They're keeping Brut in business I can tell ya! The fumes!
KAREN	Ssshhhh.
ROB	I wouldn't light a fag in there!
KAREN	They might hear ya.
ROB	I wouldn't light a fag in there, it might set the house on fire! You putting that stuff on or off? (*The make-up.*)
KAREN	You still want to come out?
ROB	Yeah! Let's go out.
KAREN	Coz if you like we can stay in. I'm not fussed. *Pause.*
ROB	When did you get back?
KAREN	You were in the garden.
ROB	You came straight upstairs?
KAREN	Long day.
ROB	Boring was it?
KAREN	Why should it be boring? *Beat.*
ROB	Leon reckons he's gonna pull tonight.

64

KAREN	Leave him alone.
ROB	What if he did drag some poor girl back here?
KAREN	You know how he is.
ROB	There's something about him It's not right.
KAREN	He'll work it out for himself.
ROB	That's what I'm worried about.
	Long pause. KAREN *has finished her make-up.* *She turns to* ROB, *to have a Conversation.*
KAREN	What d'you reckon about getting another car?
ROB	What kind of car?
KAREN	For when I move office
ROB	A city runner?
KAREN	So's you don't have to drop me off all the time
ROB	A nice little two-door runaround you're after?
KAREN	We can afford it. My wages are going up. My wages are for luxuries. Why should I rely on you to pick me up? I want to go places on my own.
ROB	What kinda places? We'll see
KAREN	We'll see, will we?
ROB	Yeah.
KAREN	We'll see, will we? ROB *sits down next to her.*
ROB	We'll see *He starts kissing her.*
KAREN	Don't. Rob.
	He withdraws.
ROB	We can't buy another car
KAREN	No?
ROB	I can't buy you a car

KAREN	Why not?
	Beat.
ROB	Because we're all gonna go on strike
	That's the way it's heading.
KAREN	I don't think I heard you properly, Rob.
	You are going on a *what?*
ROB	We're going on strike.
KAREN	You promised me. Rob.
	We discussed this over glasses of wine, expensive wine . . . at dinner parties.
	You were very loud.
	You were loud about your admiration for the Iron Lady, how she was the best thing that ever happened to this country. You wore your politics on your sleeve, Rob.
	'I look after my own, that's my first priority.'
ROB	This is my own!
KAREN	You are not a coalminer, Rob
ROB	They *are* my own
KAREN	With coal on your fucking face
ROB	Mickey, Trevor
KAREN	*You wear a tie, now.*
ROB	We're in it together. Dave, Jock, Alan. I can't shit on them!
	We gave an inch and the bastards took a mile.
	And it's not just the blokes on the floor.
	It's all joined up, that's what I've been realising.
	LEON *and* STEVEN *enter, all done up for the evening.*
KAREN	Oh, you look nice.
LEON	We're off.
KAREN	Have you got Leon's Lauren jumper on, Steve?
STEVEN	No.
LEON	He's got the same one as me.
KAREN	Well, have fun, boys
STEVEN	Thanks
KAREN	Be good.

LEON	(*To* ROB.) See ya, mate.
	ROB *flinches*.
ROB	Yeah.
	LEON *and* STEVEN *exit*.
	They called us in today. All the supervisors. Offered us . . . a five-figure sum If we took redundancy now.
KAREN	What kind of five-figure sum?
ROB	It don't matter what kind
KAREN	Ten grand? Fifty grand? . . . Well?
ROB	Twenty grand.
KAREN	You turned that down?
ROB	I'm not going to shit on my boys.
KAREN	You could start up with that. That's what you've always wanted. To go out on your own. The factory is *closing*. Maybe not this year. But it's the *way* things are *going*. They'll give you fuck all when that happens. I ain't gonna provide for you, Rob.
ROB	I love you.
KAREN	You've always wanted to start up something. Go into business. You'd be good at that. You won't get many chances.
ROB	They reckon the markets are changing, Karen. We're coming out of the slump. The lights are coming on. In India, people will be buying. They reckon hundreds of millions of Indians with enough money to buy a car. It's gonna be incredible.
	KAREN *begins to put her make-up on, then grabs her make-up bag and gets up.*
KAREN	Actually I was putting my make-up on, Rob
ROB	Just a couple more years.

KAREN	I'm going out.
ROB	Where?
KAREN	Some people at work are having a Christmas party.
ROB	You already had that.
KAREN	It's been a good year. They're having another one.

She exits. ROB takes stock. He thinks some more. He sits down and looks at himself in KAREN's mirror.

He goes to pick up the phone, and puts a little pair of spectacles on to read his address book. He finds a number. He dials a number.

ROB	Terry It's Rob, mate. You alright? Yeah not so bad, yerself? Yeah, not so bad, yerself Yeah Yeah, sorry to call you at home. No no, I'm fine. No, all it is . . .

Are you sitting down mate?
Can I speak to you in confidence?

Scene Fifteen

Braveheart

LEON at the strip of green, by a ditch. It is snowing. Winter coats. Cans of beer.

LEON	So we go to the border The strip of green Where the London Road meets Whalebone Lane. The border, the end of London. A farm Some scrubland. A ditch that cuts across it.

You gather in clumps along the bank
Drinkin just to keep warm
And when you run out, Steve goes on a mission
   to the offey.
I bet he'll get served!

And the snow's gone
But as we speak the mist on our breath collides.
And our mouths taste bitter

And on this night anything could happen
You could fall in love
You could get pregnant
You could smoke till your lungs are like caviar.

And over there
They're playing Top Trumps for beats on the arm.

And over there
Tim and Jenny Tyler have gone into the bushes.

He breathes deeply. He closes his eyes.

And way over there, as the ditch curves by the
    bridge.
Amy's just arrived with three blokes in tow.
Two blokes and the new kid.
And then it becomes clear to you what Steve was
    talking about.

He sees STEVEN *approach with great determin-
ation, carrying a blue polythene bag full of booze.*

D'you get em then?
I bet he didn't even ask you.

STEVEN   He didn't even ask me.

          STEVEN *tosses the booze onto the floor.*

LEON   You always get served.

STEVEN   Yeah, me and Mr Patel.

LEON   You're like 'that'.

STEVEN   We were chatting.

LEON   Were ya?

STEVEN   You little fucking shit you've been quiet haven't ya?

LEON   What?

STEVEN   Your old man

LEON   What?

STEVEN   It's all over the fucking town, mate.

LEON   What?

STEVEN   You don't know?

LEON	No.
STEVEN	He took redundancy.
	Pause.
LEON	That's a lie.
STEVEN	You sayin I'm lying, Lee?
LEON	He wouldn't do that.
STEVEN	He always thought he was better.
LEON	I swear, Steve.
STEVEN	Lordin it round in a fucking suit, course he's the first to take the money
LEON	He don't
STEVEN	How else is he gonna get you a moped?
LEON	Steve
STEVEN	Don't speak to me
LEON	Mate
STEVEN	Fuck off
LEON	Please, Steve.
STEVEN	Fuck off back to Daddy. Spoilt little Go on, run back home You look like you're gonna cry
LEON	Not gonna cry.
STEVEN	Or piss yourself
	Pause. LEON *suddenly realigns his loyalties.*
LEON	Have a look over there, Steve. Over by the bridge
	STEVEN *suddenly realigns his emotions.*
STEVEN	What's she doing?
LEON	I dunno, can't make it out.
STEVEN	Is he talking to her?
LEON	I dunno, looks like it
STEVEN	Looks like she's talking to him
LEON	It's probably only talking
STEVEN	Probably?

	Beat. STEVEN *breathes deeply, trying not to crumble.*
	She's
LEON	Nah
STEVEN	I knew there was someone.
LEON	It probably don't mean nothing.
STEVEN	I'll kick his Paki head in.
	Beat.
LEON	What?
STEVEN	I'll fuckin kill him.
	STEVEN *tries to run off.* LEON *restrains him.*
LEON	What are you doing? It's not worth it, Steve. It's not worth it.

STEVEN *shrugs* LEON *off, propelling him into the ditch, and charges off.* LEON *is wet through and freezing. But something is changing in the atmosphere.*

Oi! Steve!
Steve

LEON *notices what's going on, off.*

Oh fucking hell.
Whatchoo doing, mate? You can't take on Steve!

LEON *picks up a bottle of clear white cider from the bag, twists it, and has a swig. He follows the fight, as something weird is happening, a build-up to something. He puts the bottle down.*

That's it, mate, hit him!
Fuckin hell
Fuckin hell

What follows is a definite metaphysical shift – into a stylised, physical place without regular laws. Perhaps something (some music, some magic) has already been leading up to it. But now BANG.

STEVEN *is walloped onstage by an extraordinary source of propulsion – causing him to be almost – if not entirely – in flight. At any rate, his legs need*

71

to catch up with his body, and he is clutching his jaw.

DANNY calmly follows him, and socks him again, forcing him another three or four metres and onto the floor, near the blue polythene bag. DANNY seems to have developed an Essex accent since the afternoon.

DANNY   Come on!
Come on, you yellow bastard, putcha fists up.

Come on, Sunshine!

STEVEN   Go on, Lee, hit him.
Go on.

LEON   Fuck off, Steve

STEVEN   (*To* DANNY, *of* LEON.)
I don't know what he's getting all funny for, he
    was the one who set me onto you.

STEVEN gathers the cider bottle, and swigs from it like he's a Viking. He replaces the cap. Now he has a weapon.

He stands. He raises the bottle above his head, like a Viking club. Something charges inside it. Like it contains lightning.

Thunder.

LEON   No

STEVEN   Come on then!

LEON   It's not worth it, Steve!

STEVEN   Fuck off, Leon

LEON   Play fair!

LEON approaches STEVEN, and STEVEN swings at LEON, at precisely the moment when there is lightning. LEON backs off.

DANNY   Come on then!

STEVEN charges at DANNY. There is even stronger lightning as STEVEN smashes the bottle down between DANNY's eyes.

DANNY is propelled into the ditch. STEVEN follows DANNY into the ditch, grabs DANNY's hair, pulls his head up then plunges it down, at

> *precisely the moment when a fuckload of water*
> *falls from the sky.*

> *STEVEN holds DANNY's head down. Then, job*
> *done, he gets out of the ditch. DANNY does not*
> *move.*

LEON   What the fuck have you done?

> *STEVEN isn't sure.*

Call an ambulance
Call an ambulance
Well GO, THEN!
Run
Run!

> *STEVEN runs. LEON assesses the job at hand.*

Come on, Leon.
Come on, mate

> *He sprints into the ditch like a number one action*
> *hero.*

> *A fuckload of water falls from the sky.*

> *Soon he is dragging DANNY onstage. Both of*
> *them are soaking wet and freezing. DANNY is in*
> *pain.*

Alright alright alright, mate.

DANNY   Come on!

LEON   It's only water!

DANNY   I'll fuckin take you on!

LEON   I'm not gonna hit you!
I'm not gonna touch you.

An ambulance is on its way.

> *And LEON is breathing, right on top of DANNY.*

I just wanna know that you're breathing.
I thought you'd drowned.

> *Beat.*

I don't think you need mouth to mouth

> *A moment. DANNY drifts away.*

Oh shit.

Don't take this the wrong way.

73

LEON *tries CPR. A moment.*

Listen
New Kid on the Block
What's your name?

LEON *fumbles in* DANNY's *jacket. Finds his wallet. Finds a name.*

No, I just want your name. Danny. Can you hear me, Danny?

DANNY *can, groggily.*

Yeah?
Say 'Yes mate.'

DANNY Yes mate

LEON That's right.
You put up a good fight but he played dirty.

The sound and light of an ambulance.

Can you hear that? You'll be alright soon.

(*To the paramedics.*) Oi!
Here y'are!

(*To* DANNY.) You sank, mate
Right down.

I pulled you up.

I pulled you up, mate.

The lights and siren of an ambulance grow near.

End of Act One.

ACT TWO: The Dolphin

Scene Sixteen

Hospital

A waiting room, Oldchurch Hospital, Romford, about 10.30 p.m.
DANNY lies on a hospital bed, unconscious. He is strapped to
the kind of backboard used to treat concussion. On a chair hangs
the motorcyclist's jacket. ANNIE, in a thick coat, keeps watch.

ANNIE   You know . . . you look so like your dad.

             Those (*The jacket.*) were his leathers. I reckon you
             knew that.

             He used to be ever-so-into his bikes.

             When he turned seventeen he wanted one. So
             he and Bill they went out and found an Old
             Enfield. Used to talk about it all the time, that's
             what got me into it.

             ANNIE *gets a photograph out of her purse.*

             I always keep this.
             Look, there he is.
             And me
             It all still fits.
             I still wear those.
             I can't stop thinking about him.

             LEON *enters, with a blanket round his shoulders.*

LEON   There's still nobody answering.

ANNIE   Fuckssake

LEON   It's bad, that.

ANNIE   Where is she? What a fucking night.
             Never thought I'd spend it making your
             acquaintance.

LEON   I didn't have to stay.

ANNIE   You ain't shown any signs of going though, have ya?

LEON   I could have walked off

ANNIE	So why didn't ya? What kind of guilt compels you? Did you start it? I weren't born yesterday, I know what you lot are like. Causing trouble.
LEON	I don't cause trouble.
ANNIE	And you have to pick on this one, don't you? The poor little thing, he couldn't have had a worse year.

LEON	You said.
	I didn't know that. He kept all that quiet though
	    God knows it's nothing to be ashamed of. It
	    don't matter where he's from, I wouldn't hurt him.

ANNIE	I want to know who's responsible. Why I get a phone call *from the police*. 'There's been an assault. The mother's not answering so we're giving you a try.' How'd they even get my number?
LEON	It was in his wallet.
ANNIE	Was it?
LEON	Yeah.
	Beat.
ANNIE	Yeah, well, I want to know who's responsible. Draggin me out in the cold. I want you to tell me what happened.
LEON	Ah 'S a long story.
ANNIE	Were you drunk?
LEON	No.
ANNIE	How comes I can smell it on ya? Lookin a state, I've seen ya. Tennants Super.
LEON	Heineken

ANNIE	Silly prat, all it takes is a fuckin Bailey's and you
	    boys are on the floor being sick and singin
	    fuckin sea shanties.
	Was he drunk?

LEON	No
	He wasn't drunk
	The problem was, was this bloke.
ANNIE	I'll want his name
LEON	He shall remain nameless.
ANNIE	Oh, shall he?
LEON	He's havin an hard time of it: love life, family
ANNIE	Don't excuse it.
LEON	I'm not excusing it.
ANNIE	Friend of yours, is he?
LEON	I don't know any more.
ANNIE	Well, I'll want his name.

DANNY *wakes up*.

DANNY	Whooaahh.
ANNIE	You're alright, love.
	There's been no damage.
	You ain't woke up in a different universe.
DANNY	Feels like it.
ANNIE	You were thumped, hard, apparently.
	Concussed and knocked into a bit of water.
	This is Oldchurch Hospital, and you can thank your lucky stars to be in a bed. The nurse outside is itching to get you out coz some boy needs his stomach pumped but I told her. There could be complications. I told her you're gonna stay here as long as you want. They ain't gonna touch my nephew.
DANNY	I was winning.
ANNIE	Were ya?
LEON	You were. You got a couple on his chin.
DANNY	Then he gets out this massive bottle
LEON	Two litres, full up.
DANNY	What was it?
LEON	White Lightning
DANNY	Felt like it.

LEON	Took you right between the eyes.
DANNY	Where's my mum?
ANNIE	Your mum.

Beat.

Think of me as your fairy godmother.
Here y'are, let me prop you up.
That's right.

I like your jacket.
It's durable, that.

LEON	It suits ya.

ANNIE	We tried calling your mum.
	We left messages.
	Nobody picked up. Time and time again.
	Where she is at this hour I don't know, or who
	    she's with, it's a scandal.
	So when you're ready – there's no rush.
	I can take you to mine tonight.
	There's a spare bedroom.
	Would you like that?
	And tomorra. I could take you out on the bike.
	    A trip out to Essex or something?

DANNY	What are you doing here?
ANNIE	You had my number in your wallet!

You can stay with me tonight.

DANNY	No
ANNIE	You need observing.
DANNY	What do you care?
ANNIE	We always cared about you – your nan and me. We always cared. We sent cards at birthdays. We sent Advent calendars.

Beat.

I better find a nurse – tell her you're back in this
    world.
Can I get anyone a cup a tea?
No?

I tell you you've got a friend here in Leon, Danny

She exits.

LEON	That stupid wanker Steve, I can't believe it.
	Bang out of order
	I never seen him like that
DANNY	It's alright.
LEON	It's not alright
DANNY	Coz at the end of the day
LEON	At the end of the day he faces criminal charges.

Beat.

You said you was from central London, didn't
    you? The inner city, I s'pose.
My grandad. He was from central London. Well,
    East End really.
It's more or less in the middle.
He ended up doing six months hard labour.
He was a salesman. He sold housewives
    ditchweed – told them it was Japanese roses.

It's a bit shit innit, here?
Well, it's alright.

No, it's shit. I look at it, my heart goes grey.
What was it like, in the centre?

He goes over to the window.

You wanna sweet?

DANNY	Yeah, alright. What kind?
LEON	Lovehearts.
DANNY	Go on then.

*DANNY takes one. LEON goes over to the
window.*

LEON	There used to be a swimming pool.
	The Dolphin.
	I used to like going.
	Wave-splash, everything.
	But they closed it.
	The building's still there – this dirty glass pyramid
	wiv an hole in the roof.
	No one goes in it now.
	I used to think it might be haunted or full a
	pharaohs.
	Wish we had something proper like that here
	though.

Something really ancient.
You know, a proper pyramid.
A castle or something.
I get a bit carried away sometimes.
I let my imagination run away with me.
I mean – you might think this is stupid.
But just think, right, if one day a castle grew up
out the Dolphin. And suddenly we had a castle.
It would be wicked. Coz then we have a bit of
history. I mean people would come here, if we
had a castle. Is that stupid?

DANNY   No.

LEON   It's a bit.

DANNY   No. It's not.

LEON   It's a bit gay. Nah it ain't not proper gay.

               Once we went on an exchange trip to this town
               in France.
               And it was mostly taking the piss and trying to
               pull the girls and get fags and stuff.
               And most of the town was a shithole to be fair.
               But in the middle of the town they had this fuck-
               off massive property; turrets; lovely. A
               'Chateau'.
               And Michael Pott nearly set the fuckin thing on
               fire.
               Point was:
               I'd have been sorry to see that burn down if I lived
               there.
               But here

DANNY   You just have to pretend, don't you?
               Pretend you have big buildings. Pretend that
               tomorrow there'll . . . there'll

LEON   Be a coachload of French tourists coming to

DANNY   Take the piss

LEON   Set everything on fire!

DANNY   That's right.

LEON   Listen, could I hold your hand?
               I've always wanted to hold someone's hand in a
               hospital . . .

               Sorry, forget it.

	Listen . . . you don't need to worry any more.
	I'll look after you if you like
DANNY	I'm fine
LEON	You sure?
DANNY	It's weird, I'm feeling blinding. Can you get this thing off? (*The backboard, the neck restraint.*)
LEON	You sure?
DANNY	Yeah
LEON	There could be complications.
DANNY	It's not complicated.
	Beat.
LEON	They did all sortsa tests
DANNY	What kind?
LEON	Your vital signs.
DANNY	Let's get out of here.
LEON	What about your aunt?
DANNY	She'll work it out.
LEON	You can come round mine
DANNY	Yeah?
LEON	It's close! Nah, it won't be no trouble. My dad'll be out late. Pictures then dancing. We can get some dry clothes on you. You can borrow some of mine. Have a few beers and play Championship Manager. You're West Ham incha? Lewis said. I'm West Ham. Me dad's West Ham. I promised my dad I'd bring a friend home.
DANNY	My dad's West Ham
LEON	Yeah?
DANNY	Yeah
LEON	You sure?
DANNY	Course.

	Beat.
LEON	Your auntie told me, mate.
	My heart goes out to you.
	DANNY *gets up.*
	No, it's alright. I understand.
DANNY	Come on then.
LEON	What about your auntie?
DANNY	She'll survive, won't she?

Scene Seventeen

Clubland

RUKHSANA *in Romford's clubland, near the market square, around 11 p.m. Music from the 1990s, noise, lights. RUKHSANA holds a blue polystyrene bag, containing ingredients for a meal. She walks along, amazed by the spectacle. From the opposite direction staggers* STEVEN, *holding a near-empty two-litre bottle. He is giddy on his feet, and a muddy great bruise has developed on his chin.*

STEVEN	(*To* RUKHSANA.) Excuse me
	Excuse me
	RUKHSANA *is unafraid.*
RUKHSANA	Yes?
STEVEN	Are you scared?
RUKHSANA	No
STEVEN	Buy some more of this (*Booze.*) for me?
	I'll give you the money.
	I am eighteen, I just left my ID at home
RUKHSANA	You're too young to drink this much
	Make you sick
	Beat.
STEVEN	I can handle it
RUKHSANA	Can you?
STEVEN	I don't know.
	It's just I'm heartbroken.

RUKHSANA	Are you?
STEVEN	My girlfriend's gone with another man
RUKHSANA	Are you sure?
STEVEN	There's no smoke without fire.
RUKHSANA	Maybe it wasn't smoke.
STEVEN	You reckon?
RUKHSANA	Maybe there was no smoke. All this mist in the air. Maybe there was no smoke.
STEVEN	I hadn't thought of that.
RUKHSANA	What happened to you?
STEVEN	I got into a bit of trouble I took one smack in the face.
RUKHSANA	You poor thing
STEVEN	Has it come up bruised?
RUKHSANA	Yes. And it's bleeding a little.
STEVEN	Is it?
	RUKHSANA *gets out a tissue.*
RUKHSANA	Here
	She dabs his face, carefully.
STEVEN	Thanks
RUKHSANA	Does that hurt?
STEVEN	Yeah
RUKHSANA	Sorry
STEVEN	No, I deserve it
RUKHSANA	There.
STEVEN	What's in your bag?
RUKHSANA	Ingredients. I'm planning a meal.
STEVEN	That's good.
RUKHSANA	I'm going to cook it for my son.
STEVEN	What's he done to deserve you?
RUKHSANA	He hasn't
STEVEN	Celebration, is it?

RUKHSANA   I just got a job

STEVEN   Congratulations . . .

RUKHSANA   I don't know whether to take it or not.

            Whether I could spend the rest of my life in this
                place.

STEVEN   If it's a good job you should take it. You don't
                know when you'll get another.

RUKHSANA   No

STEVEN   They don't grow on trees

RUKHSANA   Could you spend the rest of your life here?

STEVEN   Haven't thought that far.

            I'd like to live in Florida.

RUKHSANA   I've spent all night wandering round this part of
                town.

STEVEN   What d'you reckon?

RUKHSANA   It's not so bad.

STEVEN   Could you live here all your life?

RUKHSANA   I don't know.

            Beat.

STEVEN   So maybe there isn't another man.

RUKHSANA   Maybe not.
            Maybe she's moved on. Just moved on.
            Or maybe you have a future together.
            One way or another, things will come clear.

STEVEN   You want some of this? (*The cider.*)

RUKHSANA   No thanks

STEVEN   No, it's piss anyway.

            *Somewhere near Hollywood's (a local club) one of
            the classic tunes of the 1990s kicks off.*

            Ah, tunes!

RUKHSANA   Tunes.

STEVEN   I ain't being funny or anything but do you wanna
                go Hollywood's?
            It's that club up there.
            If you come with me, they'll let us in.

RUKHSANA	Will they?
STEVEN	Yeah, you look old enough. I'll buy you a drink.
	It's . . . quite something, Hollywood's.
RUKHSANA	I think I have to get back to my son.
STEVEN	I thought he doesn't deserve it?
RUKHSANA	I promised I'd wait up for him.
STEVEN	You don't wanna start doing that it'll drive him mental.
RUKHSANA	I want to be there when he gets back.
STEVEN	Well . . . I'll buy you a drink
RUKHSANA	I won't need a drink
	But let's see if we can get you in. Hollywood's.

Scene Eighteen

Passport

Later that night. ROB's house. He has been slumped on his sofa, in his socks and with a heavy night of cans and fags behind him. LEON has just awoken him.

LEON	I thought you was going out.
ROB	So I didn't
LEON	You've been smoking
ROB	Yeah, well
LEON	You're only allowed one a year, Dad. You're allowed one cigarette a year. At Christmas.
ROB	Yeah, well, things are gonna change, Leon.
LEON	I heard about that and all.
ROB	Eh?
LEON	People have been talking about you. What's all this about you taking redundancy?
ROB	Who said that?
LEON	Steve said
ROB	That's bollocks though

LEON	Yeah?
ROB	What does he know, it's just rumours.
LEON	That's what I told him.
ROB	I wouldn't do that, Lee.
LEON	That's what I told him! Do you promise?
ROB	What you coming out with this horseshit for, Leon? Don't talk to me like this.
	DANNY enters. He is wearing some of LEON's *clothes.* ROB *is shocked.*
DANNY	What do you think?
LEON	They're smart.
DANNY	Yeah?
ROB	Er
LEON	Suits ya.
ROB	(*To* DANNY.) Alright, mate
DANNY	Alright.
ROB	Er, Leon. Can I have a word?
	They draw aside.
	What do you bring him for?
LEON	What you got against him?
ROB	He's a bit
LEON	He ain't
ROB	He's a bit
LEON	What?
ROB	You said you was bringing your girlfriend.
LEON	I didn't know you was gonna be here!
ROB	You what!
LEON	I thought you was on the razz with Mum. So why aren'tcha?
	Beat. LEON *gets the picture.*
	He got hit on the head, Dad – he had to go to hospital. His mum weren't picking up so I stayed with him.

ROB	She what?
LEON	She couldn't be found
ROB	Fucking hell, why not?
LEON	I don't know
ROB	Fuckin hell.

Aside over, as ROB *addresses* DANNY.

I'm sorry I appear a little strange, mate.
My plans for the evening fell through.
Leon told me he was bringing his girlfriend home.
But you're not Leon's girlfriend, are you?

Pause.

LEON	We thought we'd go Upton Park on Saturday.
ROB	Upton Park?
LEON	Gainst QPR.
ROB	You got your passport, have ya?
LEON	What?
ROB	I heard they'd set up customs at Seven Kings these days.
DANNY	Yeah!
ROB	It's little India, Forest Gate, Upton Park, now, innit?
DANNY	That's right.
LEON	Mate
ROB	It was a joke.
LEON	You'll need to take your passport, that was the joke.
ROB	It weren't a very good joke.
DANNY	No, it was alright.
ROB	I don't mean any offence.
DANNY	None taken.
ROB	It's just I've seen that road change, that's what I mean.
	Spent me whole life around it.
	It's a Roman road – did you know that?
	An ancient road

Into London.

It starts in the East End and makes its way right
out into Essex.

And my whole life I've lived on this road.

Me and
My
Wife

We lived in Forest Gate when we were married,
until Leon was born. Karen didn't like it – she's
from Chigwell, she don't like close quarters.

And to be fair it was no place to raise a kid and
it was changing, anyway, and we wanted to get
right out of it.

Some breathing space.

So we moved to Romford.

But my parents. They were proper cockneys – they
lived in Poplar until I was ten. And they moved
out to Forest Gate coz it was nicer!

And all the time London was creeping further and
further east.

But it hasn't got here yet. Not to Romford.

LEON   It has.

London buses we're on now.

ROB   ROMFORD IS NOT A PART OF LONDON
YOU DIPSTICK!

What are you like, Leon? What's your problem?

What is it in your brain that doesn't make the
connection? Bringing people back here.

(*To* DANNY.) It's alright, mate.

Not London. Not 'Greater London'. We're the
only town in 'Greater London' with its own
ring road. That says something.

This place was a Royal Liberty.

Do you know what that means?

It means that people were free.

Out of the city bounds.

By order of the crown.

Edward the Confessor used to come here.

For hunting.

Did you know that?

LEON   No.

ROB   He had a palace
A proper fuck-off palace.

This fantastic property.
Do you know what they used to say?
That when he was praying, the nightingales would
    fall silent.
Leon . . . this place once had *nightingales*.
Did you know that?

So now your dad's brought you to Romford, has he?

And when DANNY *speaks, he sounds like he's
from Essex.*

LEON	Dad
DANNY	He grew up here.
ROB	Did he?
DANNY	Yeah, my dad grew up here.
ROB	What's he do then, your dad?
LEON	Can I have a word, mate?
DANNY	No, it's alright, mate.
LEON	You sure?
DANNY	He's in property, my dad.
ROB	Oh yeah?
DANNY	Yeah
ROB	There's money in that.
DANNY	He's got this idea, right? That Basically There are all these places in the East End. In Hackney, Mile End, Bethnal Green, Spitalfields. And basically at the moment they're shitholes.
ROB	We know why that is
LEON	Dad!
ROB	No, I ain't being funny.
DANNY	Yeah, but the point is that the housing stock is very good.
ROB	I tell you what
	Some of it . . . is excellent.
	Beat.

DANNY	So one day
	A lot of people
	Who need to work in the city
	Or who want a bit of excitement
	Are going to renovate these places
	And they're going to be worth a lot of money.
	So my dad
	He's going to buy as many of these up as he can.
	And do em up.
ROB	You're joking.
DANNY	I'm not.
ROB	You're having a laugh.
DANNY	God's honest truth.
ROB	It's a thought, though, innit?
	Your mum . . .
	She's Indian, is she?
DANNY	Yes. She's Indian.
ROB	Nah, I'm just thinking . . .
	It's unusual, isn't it – your kind of arrangement?
	Mixing and matching.
	What does Mum do when yer dad come home?
	Does she have to cover herself up?
	Urrrgh! Urrrgh!
	White man, white man!
DANNY	Not quite!
ROB	She doesn't think we're all rapists!
DANNY	Probably!
ROB	You're alright, you!
	Does she cook, then?
DANNY	Sometimes.
ROB	She cook curry, does she?
DANNY	Yeah.
ROB	She eat it with her hands, does she?
DANNY	Yeah
ROB	I like a curry. Hot though.
DANNY	Too hot for me
ROB	Yeah?

90

DANNY	Too hot for me.
LEON	What, don't you never have chips or anything?
DANNY	Not when she's in the house.
ROB	Women. Who the fuck needs them, yeah? Fuck em. The moment you love em then they fuck you around.
	KAREN appears, unseen.
	They take off for days And nothing is said. Of course nothing is said
	The worst thing you can do, Leon. Is love a woman. I don't care what you do You can do men up the spout for all I care. But don't ever fall in love with a woman
	KAREN makes herself seen.
KAREN	Hello, Robert
	Pause.
ROB	Like this one.
KAREN	I go out for an evening and come back to find my husband has turned philosopher.
ROB	They'll kill you, Leon! You listen to me! No matter how beautiful
KAREN	Leon.
ROB	Ain't she lovely, Danny?
LEON	Dad
ROB	I asked Danny
KAREN	Rob, shut up.
ROB	Danny?
DANNY	Yes.
ROB	Yes you are. That's the answer.
	But I tell you something, Lee
	She's a fucking nightmare, she humiliates me every day of the week. Has she told you about Mr Leigh, Leon?

	With his mansion in Surrey? But he won't leave his wife
KAREN	That's not true, Lee.
LEON	No?
KAREN	I think you should let your friend call his mum, Leon.
LEON	It's through there, mate.
KAREN	You go and show him, Lee.

DANNY *and* LEON *go off to make the phone call.*

ROB	Well, I did it.
KAREN	What?
ROB	I did what you wanted. I did what you asked. You can have your car whenever you want. I hope you're happy.
KAREN	What am I supposed to say?
ROB	Say you're happy.
KAREN	Course I'm not happy. This doesn't make me happy.
ROB	It's what you wanted.
KAREN	I didn't want this. Have you told Leon?
ROB	No
KAREN	Well, you're gonna have to.
ROB	I can't
KAREN	You're gonna have to. Coz I got my own things I need to tell him.

LEON *enters.*

ROB	Is she answering?
LEON	Yes
ROB	Where has she been?
LEON	I don't know.
ROB	Was she sorry?
LEON	How am I supposed to know?

DANNY enters.

ROB	What did she say?
DANNY	She said She was cooking.
ROB	Cooking! *Beat.*
LEON	I reckon I better walk you home, mate.
KAREN	Rob'll walk you
ROB	I'll drive him.
KAREN	Don't be a fuckin moron, Rob. In your state.
LEON	It's *alright*, I'll take him
KAREN	Leon. I want you to stay here.
LEON	Why?
KAREN	Because I want to speak to you.
LEON	Yeah?
KAREN	Yeah. There's something important I want to talk about. *Pause.* Please? *Pause.*
LEON	Come on, Danny.
KAREN	Leon.
ROB	Come on, boys
KAREN	Lee.
LEON	Let's go.

He exits. DANNY *follows.* ROB *follows.*

Scene Nineteen

Family Recipe

RUKHSANA *over a hob. Cooking khichiri. There are two pots.*

| RUKHSANA | The pot had been simmering
The rice, the beans, the spinach, the ginger
For maybe an hour before I checked the messages. |

93

And then the phone rang
When I got back it was sticky
But that was no problem!
I just added water. You can see . . .

She shows the pot.

Then in a frying pan I added asafetida first, then
  cumin seeds, and onion.
Cumin, coriander, cayenne followed. I stir fried

Its scent pulled me home.

She adds the contents of the frying pan to the pot.

Then you add the contents into the pot of rice and
  beans, cover
And there it is
It'll cook for five minutes then I'll pick out the
  ginger.

I'm so hungry I want to taste it now.
But I have to hold my nerve.
And think about my poor angry boy.
I'm so hungry, but I won't break my resolve.
My mothers khichiri
An ancient recipe.
The thing she made
The day I left home.
The last time I saw her, 1977.

Poor bruised son

A key in the door. She hears. Dread.

Ach . . .
How could I have known this would happen?

ROB   (*Off.*) So where is she?

RUKHSANA   I used to be a good mother.

             ROB *storms in.*

             Where is she?

ROB   Did you not listen to any of those messages?

RUKHSANA   Where is he? Danny.

             DANNY *enters. They don't hug.*

             I thought they'd have put you in some kind of
             support.

DANNY   They called you over and over.

RUKHSANA	It's good you're up and walking.
ROB	No remorse.
LEON	Dad
ROB	And you've just been calmly cookin this stinking what do you call this?
RUKHSANA	Khichiri
DANNY	(*Imitating the accent.*) 'Khichiri'
ROB	Ha!
DANNY	Velly nice!
ROB	Ha!
LEON	It smells quite nice to me.
ROB	Oh fuck off, Leon, no one asked you to come along. Eh Danny? *To* RUKHSANA. Your son could have been killed and you seem completely unconcerned. Are you even listening to me?
RUKHSANA	Sit down.
ROB	No, I'll stand.
RUKHSANA	What could I possibly have done? If I had been at home?
DANNY	You would have been there. So who was it?
RUKHSANA	What?
DANNY	Who was you with?
RUKHSANA	Who 'was' you with, why are you speaking like this?
DANNY	What you taking the piss for?
ROB	He could have been killed.
DANNY	What are you taking the piss for, Mum? *Beat.*
LEON	I can't listen to this.
ROB	What?

DANNY	What's wrong?
LEON	Can we find somewhere quiet?
DANNY	Why?
LEON	I don't have the head for it.
	Beat.
DANNY	If you want, you can go in my bedroom.
LEON	Yeah?
DANNY	If you want.
LEON	Will you come with?
ROB	Just fuck off out of it, Leon.
	Pause. LEON *goes into* DANNY*'s bedroom.*
	So where were you?
	Beat.
RUKHSANA	It's no secret. I got offered the job, Danny.
	It's not a bad job, good terms, a good company. Small but ambitious.

	They're going to target their product
	Top secret
	At the Indian middle classes
	Because you don't get markets like that here.
	Hundreds of millions of middle-class Indians
	   with enough money to spend. In only a few
	   years' time.

	And I was trying to think about whether I want
	   to take it.
	Whether I want to live in this country at all.
	Or whether we'd be happier where the real
	   opportunities are.

DANNY	What?
RUKHSANA	I've been thinking about moving back to Bombay.
ROB	That's ridiculous.
RUKHSANA	Is it?
ROB	It's ridiculous you're even discussing this. Most people from where you're from would give their front teeth to have what you've got here.

RUKHSANA	Why do you assume I am privileged to live in a place I do not love?
	I want to go back to my home. I want to know my family. Danny . . . has never met his grandparents. We're going to visit them. What about that, Danny?
DANNY	I'm not going.
RUKHSANA	You want to stay in a place like this?
DANNY	Yes.
RUKHSANA	Why?
DANNY	Because this is where I'm from.
ROB	Tell me, what does your husband think about this?
RUKHSANA	What he *thought* was the *problem*.
ROB	Well, that's it, isn't it – that's what it's like with the lot of you!
RUKHSANA	The lot of who?
ROB	He's a local man, isn't he?
DANNY	Rob
RUKHSANA	He was local
ROB	He's got ideas about the world.
DANNY	I'm going
RUKHSANA	He did have ideas about the world
	DANNY *tries to move off quickly to his bedroom.*
	Danny!
	RUKHSANA *catches him but he flings her off and makes for the bedroom.*
	What has he said to you? About my husband? What has he said?
	Danny!
ROB	He's in property, isn't he? Development.
	Pause.
RUKHSANA	He's dead.
	He was killed. A few months ago. An accident. And for some reason coming to this country seemed to be the right thing to do.

	Why would Danny make that up?
	My husband . . . he suspected me.
ROB	Was he right?
RUKHSANA	I wasn't having an affair. No.
ROB	Yet all the signs were there?
RUKHSANA	I don't know

ROB sits down, with his head in his hands.

ROB	I'm so sorry. I'm I'm not normally like this. I think my wife's about to leave me.
RUKHSANA	Then perhaps you should go and make sure?
	Can you fetch your son? I'm not sure I can face them.

ROB gets up.

It's first on the right. (DANNY's *bedroom*.)

He disappears in the direction of DANNY's *room.*
RUKHSANA *takes stock.*

ROB reappears. Smiling, almost.

ROB	You'll never believe this.
RUKHSANA	What is it?
ROB	They've done a runner. The two of em? The window's open, they must have climbed out . . .
	I don't blame them.
RUKHSANA	No!

They laugh. Relief, somehow.

Are you hungry?

ROB	Starving.
RUKHSANA	I could put some chips in.
ROB	You got chips?
RUKHSANA	Yes
ROB	No, I want what smells so nice. Khichiri.

	Is it hot?
	I mean spicy hot.
RUKHSANA	No. It's . . . well I suppose you could say it's quite bland.
ROB	I love my wife so much.

RUKHSANA takes the ginger out of the pot. She places a serving of khichiri on ROB's place.

Pause.

Danny said you, er
You, er
Ate with your hands

RUKHSANA	Did he?
	Some people do
ROB	Well if it's no trouble / I'll
RUKHSANA	Have a go
ROB	Oh?
RUKHSANA	Just once. Have a go with your hands, there's nothing wrong with it

Beat.

ROB	Won't kill me, will it?
RUKHSANA	That's right
	(*She mimes.*) You sweep up like this.
	Use your thumb
	Push the rice upwards into your mouth.

She demonstrates, without rice. ROB sweeps up the khichiri with his left hand.

ROB	OK.
RUKHSANA	Use your right hand.
ROB	Why?
RUKHSANA	The left hand is for wiping your bottom.

Me, I prefer a knife and fork.

She gets up.

| ROB | You! |

They laugh. ROB eats. RUKHSANA serves herself some. They eat hungrily.

This is alright, this.

RUKHSANA   (*Her mouth full.*) Mmm.

ROB   Really tasty.
A recipe passed down the generations?

RUKHSANA   Yes.

ROB   Somebody's gonna be a lucky man one day.

Funny . . . eating with your hands.
Like
Did you ever go barefoot in the mud?
Squishing about?

RUKHSANA   Yes.

ROB   Some fantastic places when I was a kid.

ROB *is suffering from some strange inaction. And it is to do with* RUKHSANA.

Am I going to have to go in a minute?

RUKHSANA   No.

ROB   And what should we do about
Our children?
If they don't come back?
If they're not back by morning.

RUKHSANA   We'll leave no stone unturned

But let's just eat, for a minute . . .

ROB   That's right.

RUKHSANA   'That's right.' You sound just like my husband.

Beat. They eat.

Scene Twenty

The Sky at Night

DANNY *and* LEON. *The strip of green, a few hours later that evening.*

LEON   (So you go to the border
The strip of green
The place by the burnt-out house
The site of the old tollgate
Where the London Road meets Whalebone Lane
The border, the end of London.)

DANNY *points at Canary Wharf.*

DANNY	I didn't know you could see it from here.
LEON	It looks better at night, dunnit? Beautiful.
DANNY	All the light in it. At four in the morning, still all lit. Come on. We could walk there. We could.
LEON	No mate.
DANNY	We could.
LEON	I'm not going any further.
DANNY	Why?
	Pause.
	You cold?
LEON	It's not that.
DANNY	You can have my coat.
LEON	It's alright.
DANNY	I don't mind.
	I fancy another fight. I could have beat him.
LEON	You could
DANNY	You punched me in the stomach.
LEON	I had to.
DANNY	Why?
LEON	I was absolutely terrified.
	I can't stop thinking about my mum.
DANNY	Not worth thinking about.
LEON	It is.
DANNY	You still got your dad.
LEON	Yeah.
DANNY	He'll look after ya.
LEON	Will he?
DANNY	Yeah.
LEON	D'you wanna ciggie, Dan?
DANNY	You'll get cancer.

LEON	I don't get cancer.

DANNY gasps in admiration. They light up. They blow streams of smoke that collide like a nuclear explosion.

DANNY	Look at that
LEON	Like an atom bomb
DANNY	Tell us a secret
LEON	What kind?
DANNY	Any kind you like.
LEON	Can I trust you?
DANNY	Yeah

Beat.

LEON	I used to piss myself
DANNY	You're joking!
LEON	I'm not joking. No. I get so confused I can't control it. Panicked. I thought it'd stop when I grew up, but now I'm nearly there. Are you becoming unsure about me?
DANNY	No
LEON	Sure?
DANNY	Yeah, I'm sure.

Scene Twenty-One

Search Party

The Dolphin/marketplace. ROB and RUKHSANA enter. The clubbers have gone home. The market place is quiet.

ROB	Not a soul
RUKHSANA	Should have seen it a few hours ago.
ROB	Tell me about it.
RUKHSANA	I don't think we're going to find them.
ROB	They'll be alright.
RUKHSANA	It's so cold.

ROB	At least it's stopped snowing.
RUKHSANA	He's weak.
ROB	Don't worry about that.
RUKHSANA	No?
ROB	Leon'll look after him.
RUKHSANA	Are you sure?
ROB	I'm sure. He's a good boy I'm sure. I've already lost My wife today. And I chucked in my job. So it'd be fucking carelessness to lose anyone else.
RUKHSANA	I don't know what to do.
ROB	No
RUKHSANA	This fear that's growing.
ROB	I know.
RUKHSANA	Cold.
ROB	Come here, then.

They hug. ROB *considers a cheeky swooping snog but thinks better of it.*

RUKHSANA	I want to call my mother. Maybe she'll know what to do. They'll all be awake now, it's morning there. I want to say I'm going to take her grandson to see her
ROB	You really leaving?
RUKHSANA	I think so
ROB	I mean I'm even a bit sad
	You know what I mean?
RUKHSANA	You've given me the whole tour!
ROB	Here y'are. You see that? That pyramid behind the roundabout? That's called the Dolphin. Our contribution to the architecture of the world. A derelict swimming pool. It won awards.

It was alright when it was working. It had a
  wave-splash.
Blinding.
I used to take Leon when he was this high.

Then the roof started fallin to pieces. The council
  wouldn't pay to keep it going.
Tories.
 I voted Conservative the last four times and I
  reckon I've been made a mug.

Pause.

RUKHSANA You know what it reminds me of?
It reminds me of the top of the Canary Wharf
  tower.
The pyramid on top.
It's like when they built Canary Wharf they copied
  this.

You know what they should do?
Someone should light it up. And keep the lights
  on all night.

ROB That's an idea

RUKHSANA At least for Christmas.

ROB What did you think of me when I stormed in?
Bet you thought I was a caveman?

RUKHSANA I married a man from here.

Beat.

ROB I'm not like him, am I?

RUKHSANA No.

ROB It crossed my mind.

RUKHSANA Not when I knew him, no.

ROB Good.
Listen
Don't get me wrong
I mean given my circumstances it might seem a
  bit funny, but
If you wanted
I could take you right out into Essex, in the car.
Tomorrow maybe
Show you the country.

Listen, would you like a fag?

RUKHSANA Yeah, OK.

104

ROB	I've started going out in the garden late at night and hope she doesn't notice

They spark up.

RUKHSANA	She'll know
ROB	Yeah?
RUKHSANA	Well, you won't need to hide any more.
ROB	Small mercies, ay?
RUKHSANA	There aren't many nights like this, are there?
ROB	No
RUKHSANA	No.

She exhales, he exhales – two streams of smoke that collide like an atom bomb.

Scene Twenty-Two

The Pink Room 2

The Pink Room, the same evening. From somewhere outside a fluorescent Christmas reindeer buzzes. Hanging from the ceiling is KAREN's birthday dress. She has left it behind. There are still assorted cosmetics on the dresser. LEON and DANNY enter.

LEON	This is it. This is where they sleep.

He examines the dresser.

She never goes out without make-up.
Look there's still some here!
She wouldn't leave her make-up behind would she?

The bedstead, they got last year in the sale
And she loves it.
He sleeps on the right and she's on the left.
She's the one who snores.
When I was little I used to crawl in
Make a gap between them.

This rack.
It used to be bursting with clothes.

That dress.
He gave her that for her birthday.

She must have left it on purpose.

How could she, you know? He was alright, wasn't he?

	She's definitely gone, hasn't she?
	Listen, Danny, can I trust you? And if I can't that's fine, it don't make no difference.
DANNY	You can trust me.
LEON	It's a bit weird. No it's not, it's not weird. It's OK.
DANNY	Go on.
LEON	You sure?
DANNY	Yeah.
LEON	OK

LEON *picks up some make-up*.

	Can you put this on me? Seriously.
DANNY	What, this?
LEON	There's no harm in it.
DANNY	No, I know.
LEON	Cosmetics.
DANNY	Yeah.
LEON	Changes things.
	You take that sponge there.
DANNY	What if somebody comes?
LEON	It don't matter. That's important. It doesn't matter.

DANNY *takes up a sponge. It's the sponge you use for foundation.*

And you can do it slowly.

DANNY *applies it, slowly. Quite a pale colour. He holds* LEON's *face.*

There's no rush.

DANNY *continues applying it.*

The thing with this is

You have to hold your nerve

Because if you don't

And you cave in

You'll die

DANNY *holds* LEON*'s face. He kisses* LEON, *awkwardly, rigidly. For a time nothing moves, but then* LEON *nudges* DANNY *away.*

DANNY   What?

LEON   No, it's alright

DANNY   Sorry

LEON   It's just I'm not

DANNY   No, I'm not!

LEON   It's alright.

DANNY   Something about tonight.

LEON   There's no problem.
          You gotta try everything once, don't ya?
          And it works or it doesn't.
          Well? Did it work?

DANNY   I don't think so.

LEON   You'll work it out.
          Here y'are. Eyeliner.

          You sure you're up for this?

DANNY   How do I do it, then?

LEON   Hold my stare

          DANNY *applies the eyeliner. The doorbell rings.*

DANNY   Oh shit.

LEON   It's alright.

DANNY   Oh fuck.

LEON   Whoever it is.
          It don't matter
          There's no shame in this.
          You go and get the door.
          And don't try and divert them.
          If they wanna see me, I'll see them.

          DANNY *exits.* LEON *breathes deeply.*

          You're *alright*, mate.

          STEVEN *enters, with* DANNY.

STEVEN   Jesus

LEON	What you looking at?
STEVEN	Nothing.
	LEON *stands up*.
LEON	No, whatchoo looking at?
STEVEN	I just didn't know you still did all that.
LEON	(*To* DANNY.) Steve used to love all this We used to dress up all the time, didn't we? Steve?
	He grew out of it. So he says.
	Beat.
	You were bang out of order.
STEVEN	I know
LEON	Danny had nothing to do with it.
STEVEN	Yeah, I know.
LEON	He could press charges
STEVEN	I know. I was bang out of order. I wouldn't blame ya. You'd be within your rights if you wanted to take this further. You don't though, do you?
DANNY	No, mate.
	Shake?
STEVEN	Yeah.
	STEVEN *reaches out his hand to shake* DANNY*'s hand.* DANNY *moves to reciprocate, but at the moment of contact he flashes it up instead, smoothing his hair.*
	LEON *laughs.* DANNY *laughs.* STEVEN *laughs.*
DANNY	No, seriously.
	DANNY *shakes* STEVEN*'s hand.*
STEVEN	Cheers.
	Pause.
LEON	I'm not finished yet.
STEVEN	Mate.

LEON	I'm not finished.
	Wait.
	Just wait
	Reverentially, LEON *takes the dress off the rack, and takes the necessary clothes off in order to change into the dress.*
	Pause. They watch LEON. STEVEN *takes* DANNY *aside.*
STEVEN	I mean
	I mean, fair play to him
	Each to his own
	But . . .
	You know what I mean?
	Beat.
DANNY	Yeah.
STEVEN	I mean, his mum wore that.
	That can't be right.
	And he's making us feel like we're the queer ones.
	He didn't use to be like this.
	Pause.
	I was wrong about you.
	You're alright.
DANNY	Thanks.
	LEON *has now completed his task.*
LEON	Well?
STEVEN	Leon.
LEON	Do you like it?
	Pause.
	What?
STEVEN	Leon
LEON	What d'ya reckon?
STEVEN	Mate.
	Pause.
LEON	Well, don't just stand there
STEVEN	Leon . . .
	I've been a dickhead to you, too . . .

109

Pause. Relief.

LEON	About my dad?
STEVEN	Yeah
LEON	That slander.
STEVEN	I shouldn't have taken it out on you.
LEON	No
STEVEN	Coz it's your dad who's the guilty one.
LEON	What?
STEVEN	I'm just warning you, mate, there's uproar

The reindeer buzzes ominously. Elsewhere a key turns in a lock.

DANNY	What's that?
LEON	What?
DANNY	Someone's come in
LEON	Nah

ROB'S VOICE

This is it.

RUKHSANA'S VOICE

It's nice.

ROB'S VOICE

Home.

It's not much.

RUKHSANA'S VOICE

It's perfect.

LEON   Oh, fucking hell.

ROB'S VOICE

Let me take your coat

RUKHSANA'S VOICE

Thank you.

STEVEN   Turn the light off!

LEON *pauses, then turns the light off.*

ROB'S VOICE

You wanna go upstairs?

Pause.

The boys scurry off to hide.

> ROB *leads* RUKHSANA *into the bedroom. They are barely visible in the light.*
>
> *They sit on the bed.*
>
> *They kiss, slowly.*
>
> *This goes on for some time.*

RUKHSANA Mmmm

ROB Mmmm

Feel like I'm fifteen years old

> *They kiss again.*
>
> ROB *begins to unbutton* RUKHSANA.
>
> *And to be fair to them, they're not really shagging.*
>
> *But* LEON *can't bear it, and begins to wail.*

Wuuuuuuaaaaagh

> ROB *dives for the light switch.*
>
> *The light comes on.*

DANNY Mum

> RUKHSANA *looks at her son.*

What have you done?

> *Everyone is visible.*
>
> *And then* LEON *pisses himself. At first, only a little bit, but gradually and improbably growing into a deluge that engulfs the characters and returns the stage to rain.*

Scene Twenty-Three

The Present Day

KAREN. *She is wearing a smart suit, and carries her little glowing model of the Docklands in the future.*

KAREN And I'll tell you what it'll be like in the future.
OK.
I got this flat in Bethnal Green.
It's nice.
Top floor.
Rob owns it.
I pay him rent. He knocks a little off, but it's still
   expensive.
He owns ten houses just around here.

She holds her model aloft.

And on one side of the building.
Is a window.
And from there I can see this amazing picture
At night.
I almost can't believe what's sprung up.

I'm alone.
But that's OK – there's enough people at work to
    take care of.
And Leon comes over
He's doing well for himself
He always had a brain.
He's got himself a girl.
We go out to a bar.
And I don't like it that he's smoking
But he buys the drinks.
He *knows* how to order drinks.
And he's all grown up.

Scene Twenty-Four

Old Enfield

DANNY *and* RUKHSANA*'s house. The trunk has gone.* ANNIE
*is packing up the boxes in the room, and stacking them up. Her
motorbike is parked outside, and her helmet rests on top of the
sink.*

A motorcyclist, helmeted, appears in the doorway.

ANNIE *turns to see the motorcyclist, much as he might have
looked nearly twenty years ago. She gazes at him, astonished.*

ANNIE	Simon?
	The motorcyclist takes his helmet off. It is DANNY.
	Oh
	Oh.
	Something just happened.
	Beat.
DANNY	Are you ready?
ANNIE	Of course. Of course you understand.
	Beat.
DANNY	Yes

Pause.

ANNIE   There's something I want you to know.
                About all that stuff.
                The way I was thinking when your dad went off.
                At that time there was a lot of pressure on resources.
                Houses, school places.
                And I'm not saying they didn't need em, the
                    Bangladeshis.

                But Mum couldn't get a council place. That's why
                    we had to move out here.
                And she'd kick off sometimes
                And they're only words, though, in't they?
                I don't think we meant any harm. Or maybe we did.
                And some of it was just jokes.
                Before he went off to university
                Simon joined in, too.
                Yes. He did.
                He did
                He didn't know better.
                He did a proper funny Indian accent, I tell you
                We used to laugh and laugh
                And it was how we were.
                But how was I to know it would leave us like this?

                Danny. There is a future. It's been proved
                Time and time again.

                ANNIE *moves off, out.* DANNY *remains, looking
                at the house.*

Scene Twenty-Five

The Dolphin

LEON *and* DANNY, *standing outside the Dolphin, all dark. They watch it. Suddenly, it lights up, gloriously.*

The End.

Other Titles in this Series

Caryl Churchill
BLUE HEART
CHURCHILL PLAYS: THREE
CHURCHILL: SHORTS
CLOUD NINE
A DREAM PLAY *after* Strindberg
DRUNK ENOUGH TO SAY I LOVE YOU?
FAR AWAY
HOTEL
ICECREAM
LIGHT SHINING IN BUCKINGHAMSHIRE
MAD FOREST
A NUMBER
THE SKRIKER
THIS IS A CHAIR
THYESTES *after* Seneca
TRAPS

Kevin Elyot
THE DAY I STOOD STILL
ELYOT: FOUR PLAYS
FORTY WINKS
MOUTH TO MOUTH
MY NIGHT WITH REG

Stella Feehily
DUCK
O GO MY MAN

Debbie Tucker Green
BORN BAD
DIRTY BUTTERFLY
STONING MARY
TRADE & GENERATIONS

Stephen Jeffreys
THE CLINK
A GOING CONCERN
I JUST STOPPED BY TO SEE THE MAN
THE LIBERTINE

Fin Kennedy
HOW TO DISAPPEAR COMPLETELY
AND NEVER BE FOUND
PROTECTION

Ayub Khan-Din
EAST IS EAST
LAST DANCE AT DUM-DUM
NOTES ON FALLING LEAVES
RAFTA, RAFTA . . .

Tony Kushner
ANGELS IN AMERICA – PARTS ONE & TWO
CAROLINE, OR CHANGE
HOMEBODY/KABUL

Owen McCafferty
CLOSING TIME
DAYS OF WINE AND ROSES *after* JP Miller
MOJO MICKYBO
SCENES FROM THE BIG PICTURE
SHOOT THE CROW

Conor McPherson
DUBLIN CAROL
McPHERSON: FOUR PLAYS
McPHERSON PLAYS: TWO
PORT AUTHORITY
THE SEAFARER
SHINING CITY
THE WEIR

Arthur Miller
AN ENEMY OF THE PEOPLE *after* Ibsen
PLAYING FOR TIME

Jack Thorne
FANNY AND FAGGOT & STACY
WHEN YOU CURE ME

Enda Walsh
BEDBOUND & MISTERMAN
DISCO PIGS & SUCKING DUBLIN
THE SMALL THINGS
THE WALWORTH FARCE

Alexandra Wood
THE ELEVENTH CAPITAL

Nicholas Wright
CRESSIDA
HIS DARK MATERIALS *after* Pullman
MRS KLEIN
THE REPORTER
THERESE RAQUIN *after* Zola
VINCENT IN BRIXTON
WRIGHT: FIVE PLAYS